30 DAYS

TO UNDERSTANDING

WHAT CHRISTIANS BELIEVE

Other books in the "30 Days" series

30 Days to Understanding the Bible
30 Days to Understanding How to Live as a Christian

30 DAYS
TO UNDERSTANDING
WHAT CHRISTIANS BELIEVE

MAX ANDERS

WORD PUBLISHING
Dallas • London • Vancouver • Melbourne

Library of Congress Cataloging-in-Publication Data

Anders, Max E., 1947–
   30 days to understanding what Christians believe / Max Anders.
     p. cm.
   ISBN 0-8499-3491-5 (pbk.)
   1. Theology, Doctrinal—Popular works.   I. Title.   II. Title: Thirty days to understanding what Christians believe.
BT77.A46   1994
230—dc20   94–5694
                                                    CIP

4 5 6 7 8 9 LBM 7 6 5 4 3 2 1

Printed in the United States of America

CONTENTS

SECTION THREE: Ten Key Words of Bible Doctrine

ACKNOWLEDGMENTS

I would like to thank Kip Jordon and Joey Paul at Word, Inc., for their encouragement of the "30 Days" series and this volume, in particular. I also thank Roxanne Brooks for her heroic contribution of typing and editing the final manuscript. I am grateful to my wife, Margie, for accommodating my preoccupation during a particularly hectic time in our lives (are such things ever convenient?) and for the skillful editorial help she contributed to this book. And finally, I thank the Lord for saving me and placing in my heart the desire to do the things He then asks me to do.

INTRODUCTION

We live in an age of feelings. Increasingly greater value is being placed on whether something makes us feel good. At the same time, there is a decreasing value on knowledge, information, and truth, with many people believing that truth is relative: "What may be true for you may not be true for me." This is devastating, however, because if there is no absolute truth, there can be no confidence that God exists. If there is no God, there is no hope. Therefore, Christians must be concerned about preserving knowledge, information, and truth.

"Cold, dead orthodoxy" has no appeal to anyone. There is no virtue in believing something that is barren and meaningless. But the Bible makes claims that, if true, are rich and profoundly meaningful. It makes it clear that if you truly believe the right things, you will experience love, joy, and peace . . . but only if you believe the right things. The quality of a person's life depends on what he or she believes, and the destiny of that person's life depends equally on what he or she believes.

All this is to say that it matters what Christians believe. It matters that Christians be well educated in the Scriptures. It matters that Christians be grounded solidly in the truth. It matters that truth is upheld, preserved, and honored. Otherwise we are vulnerable to lies that deceive and destroy.

Yet, at the same time, we live in a post-Christian era, in which much of the information about Christianity that used to be common knowledge in American culture is no longer common knowledge. Therefore, for upcoming generations, we must make the basic truths of Christianity more accessible. That is what this book is all about . . . making the most fundamental truths about God, the Bible, and salvation by grace through faith in Jesus Christ accessible to as wide an audience as possible. It is rooted deeply in the conviction that most learning is self-generated, so we must teach the basics and teach them well. Then the learner is in a position to go on to self-guided advanced learning with a solid foundation. In this way, teaching less is actually teaching more, because the learner is not overloaded up-front and defeated in the process.

I offer this book to you in the hope that you will enjoy and profit from a greater understanding of the fundamental truths of Christianity and that your walk with Christ and your understanding of Scripture will be enriched as a result.

There are three ways you can study these fundamental truths of Bible doctrine. (Note: Theology and Bible doctrine are, essentially, the same thing. Theology is the study of God and related subjects. Bible doctrine is essentially studying the teachings of the Bible and related subjects. Theologians are able to make a distinction between the terms, but for our purposes, the meanings are so similar that we will use them interchangeably.) The three ways to study are:

1. Systematic Theology

2. Biblical Theology

3. Key Theological Terms

Most books study the subject one of these three ways. In this book, we are going to do it all three ways! Let me explain the differences between the ways, in case they are new to you.

In the Systematic Theology section, you study the categories in the Bible with the broadest scope. That is, you pick the major subjects under which all other subjects fit. Commonly, the ten major subjects of systematic theology are:

The Doctrine of the Bible

The Doctrine of God the Father

The Doctrine of God the Son

The Doctrine of God the Holy Spirit

The Doctrine of Angels

The Doctrine of Man

The Doctrine of Sin

The Doctrine of Salvation

The Doctrine of the Church

The Doctrine of Future Things

Theoretically, at least, all other subjects in the Bible can be placed under one of these great categories.

There is great value in studying systematic theology because you learn to mentally categorize the information you learn, and therefore, you understand and remember the information better.

There is a limitation to systematic theology, however. The limitation is that often the Bible spends a great deal of time talking about things not covered in the broader categories of systematic theology. That's where biblical theology comes into play. Its emphasis is on trying to determine which subjects the Bible emphasizes the most. These subjects are the focus of Section 2 of this book.

For example, the subject of money is not found in systematic theology until you work your way down into the details of the categories, yet money is a very prominent theme in the Bible. In fact, there are almost two thousand direct or indirect references to money and its related issues in the Bible. A very high percentage of the teachings of Jesus deal with money. Therefore, money would be one of the major subjects you would study in biblical theology.

As another example, the subject of angels is one of the major categories in systematic theology, yet the Bible does not talk about angels nearly as much as it talks about money.

An historical analogy to these ways of studying what Christians believe would be that if you were studying the history of armed conflict in the United States, you would have to mention all the conflicts, including the War of 1812 and the Korean Conflict. That would be studying the subject of American armed conflict *systematically*.

However, if you were going to study the greatest American armed conflicts . . . the conflicts that took the greatest time, resources, and human life . . . you would barely mention the War of 1812 and you would spend a great deal of time on the Civil War, the war in which more Americans died than any other war.

That is essentially the difference. When you study something systematically, you look for *all* the existing categories, regardless of how much emphasis that category has. When you study subjects for emphasis, as biblical theology does, you try to determine which subjects are given the most weight in the Bible by virtue of the amount of time the Bible spends talking about them. It is not that there is a right way or a wrong way to study Bible doctrine. Rather, there are different ways, each of which has its strengths and weaknesses.

Key words need to be studied no matter what other ways you study doctrine. However, as a rule, in brief overviews such as this you can't get specific enough to deal with many key words. So we isolate some of the most important key words that are very important regardless of whether you are studying doctrine systematically or biblically.

True theologians may gasp at my overgeneralizations and tremble at all the things I have left out of this book. However, since I started out *not* trying to answer the question, How much does the reader need to know? but rather, How much time will the reader give me? I decided to teach whatever I thought I could teach in fifteen minutes a day for thirty days. That automatically forces the exclusion of much valuable information and creates some subjectivism in the topics dealt with.

Finally, and very importantly, this book is not intended to be the last book on doctrine you ever read. Rather, it is intended, in a sense, to be the first. After this overview, details need to be added. I would like to recommend three books for further reading and, if this is new to you, I would read them in this order: *Know What You Believe* by Paul Little (Victor Books, 1985), *Concise Theology* by James I. Packer (Tyndale, 1993), and *A Survey of Bible Doctrine* by Charles C. Ryrie (Moody, 1972).

I hope this book is helpful to you whether this information is new to you or you are a seasoned veteran and are using the book to help you organize your own thinking on the subjects or using it to teach others. To God be the glory!

TEN
GREAT
DOCTRINES
OF
SYSTEMATIC
THEOLOGY

OVERVIEW OF SECTION ONE

The Bible is more than history. If you would know the Bible, you must go beyond the historical study of its teachings . . . and taking that plunge is not easy. One day Harry Cohen, the head of Columbia Studios in Hollywood, was in a conversation with his brother Jack, who suggested to Harry that they produce a biblical epic. "What do you know about the Bible?" cried Harry. "I'll lay you fifty dollars you don't even know the Lord's Prayer." After a moment's thought, Jack began, "Now I lay me down to sleep . . ." and recited the well-known child's bedtime prayer. Harry pulled fifty dollars out of his pocket. "Well, I'll be!" he said as he handed the money to his brother. "I didn't think you knew it."

There have been so many approaches to mastering the teaching of the Bible, some more successful than others. Menelik II was emperor of Ethiopia from 1889 until 1913, and he had one eccentricity. If he felt ill, he was convinced that he had only to eat a few pages of the Bible in order to feel better. This odd behavior did him little harm as long as his literary consumption was kept at a modest level. However, in December 1913 he was recovering from a stroke when he suddenly felt extremely ill. On his instructions the complete Book of Kings was torn from the Bible and fed to him, page by page. He died before he finished.

Our approach should be more effective and less painful.

When you add all the authors and all the books of the Bible together, and then boil them down to their irreducible minimum, what does the Bible teach? What subjects does it cover, and what does it say about each subject? When you add Moses, David, Jesus, and Paul together, what did they teach about God, Christ, angels, the future? As you begin to answer these questions, you are trafficking in the subject known as "Bible doctrine."

It is difficult to get two people to agree on all points of doctrine. There is an old Irish proverb that says:

> O Lord, turn the hearts of our enemies.
> And if You can't turn their hearts,
> Then turn their ankles,
> So we can know them by their limp.

There are many people limping, in the eyes of others, over certain doctrinal distinctions. However, there is a basic body of doctrine that nearly all Christians have historically agreed upon. It is that body that we will focus upon in this section.

Depending on how finely you split the hairs, different Bible scholars have come up with different numbers of minimum subjects. For the purpose of our study, we will use ten. The ten great doctrines of systematic theology are listed below. Every teaching of the Bible is in a subdivision of one of these doctrines, or subjects.

Ten Great Doctrines of Systematic Theology

1. The Bible
2. God
3. Christ
4. Holy Spirit
5. Angels
6. Man
7. Sin
8. Salvation
9. Church
10. Future Things

As you read the following descriptions, note that, to help you remember the doctrine, a symbol has been assigned to each one.

 1. **The Bible**, symbolized by a book, deals with the origin and nature of the Scriptures. How did we get them? Are they reliable? Are they the Word of God?

 2. **God**, symbolized by the crown of a king, deals with the first person of the Trinity. Who is He? What is He like? And what is our relationship to Him?

 3. **Christ**, symbolized by the Lamb of God, deals with Jesus of Nazareth, the second person of the Trinity. Was He a man? Was He God? Is He alive today? Is He coming to earth again?

 4. **Holy Spirit**, the third person of the Trinity, is symbolized by a dove. Is He a personal being or the religious equivalent of "school spirit"?

 5. **Angels**, symbolized by angel wings and a halo, investigates the reality of the spirit world. What about guardian angels? What about demon possession and Satan worship?

 6. **Man**, symbolized by an individual, investigates the origin, nature, and destiny of humanity. Were humans created, or did they evolve? Do they have souls? Does the soul live forever?

7. **Sin**, symbolized by a bite taken out of an apple, deals with the nature of mankind's offense against God.

8. **Salvation,** symbolized by a life-saving float ring, deals with the afterlife, heaven, hell, and whether or not it is safe to die.

9. **Church**, a body of organized believers, is symbolized by a church building and investigates what the church is in the eyes of God and what its responsibilities are.

10. **Future Things**, symbolized by an hourglass, looks into biblical prophecy and what the Bible says about future events, the end of the world, and eternity.

Review

(Fill in the blanks from the options at the left.)

OPTIONS:	DOCTRINE:	DESCRIPTION:
Salvation	BIBLE	The origin and nature of the Scriptures
Christ	GOD	The first person of the Trinity
Future Things	CHRIST	The second person of the Trinity
God		
The Bible	HOLY SPIRIT	The third person of the Trinity

OPTIONS:	DOCTRINE:	DESCRIPTION:
Sin	*ANGELS*	The spirit world
Angels	*CHURCH*	Organized believers
	MAN	The origin, nature, and
Man		destiny of humanity
	SALVATION	The afterlife, heaven, hell
Church	*Sin*	Man's offense against God
Holy Spirit	*FUTURE*	Biblical prophecy

To further help you remember these ten great doctrines, notice that the order suggests a logical progression. As you read the descriptions below, write the name of the doctrine next to the corresponding number and symbol on the following chart. By following the numbers and arrows on the chart, you can see the logical progression from one doctrine to the next. This will help you remember the ten great doctrines.

1. **The Bible**
   The Bible is the foundation for what we learn about the other seven subjects, so it is first.

2. **God**
   God is the first member of the Trinity.

3. **Christ**
   Christ is the second member of the Trinity.

4. **Holy Spirit**
   The *Holy Spirit* is the third member of the Trinity.

5. **Angels**
   Angels are lower than God, but higher than man, so are placed between God and man.

6. **Man**
   Man is made in the image of God.

7. **Sin**
   Sin is man's shortcomings in God's eyes.

8. **Salvation**
   Salvation is offered by God to man through faith.

9. **Church**

Church proclaims the message of salvation.

10. **Future Things**

Future Things are a prophetic record of things that will happen in the future.

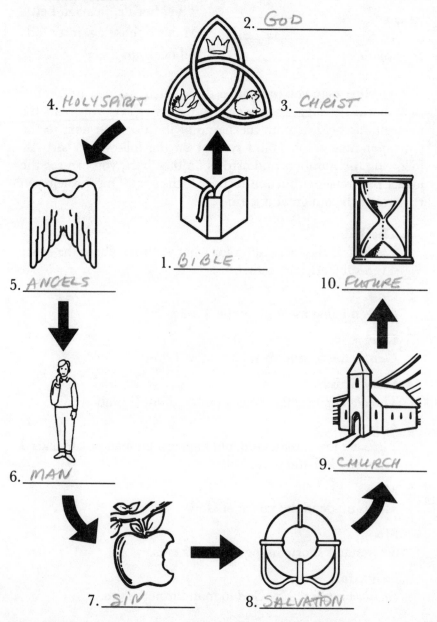

2. GOD

4. HOLY SPIRIT

3. CHRIST

1. BIBLE

5. ANGELS

10. FUTURE

6. MAN

9. CHURCH

7. SIN

8. SALVATION

Review

Ten Great Doctrines of Systematic Theology

As a final review, fill in the names of the ten doctrines from memory. See pages 5–6 to check your answers.

 1. BIBLE

 2. GOD

 3. CHRIST

 4. H SPIRIT

 5. ANGELS

 6. _MAN_

 7. _SIN_

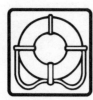 8. _SALV._

 9. _CHURCH_

 10. _ANGELS_

Now, having established a base of the ten great doctrines of systematic theology, we are ready to overview each doctrine separately in the chapters that follow.

ONE

THE DOCTRINE OF
THE BIBLE

It is not the things I don't understand
about the Bible that bother me. It's the
things I do understand.

Mark Twain

Let me tell you about the last flight of the *Lady Be Good,* an airplane, a bomber that had seen many successful wartime missions
and was out one night on a familiar bombing run. As she flew
back toward home base, the crew knew how long it usually took
to make the trip.

Tonight, however, there was a powerful tailwind hurtling
the massive craft through the air much faster than normal. As
the crew plotted their position according to their instruments,
they concluded that there must be something wrong with the
dials. Their instruments and calculations told them it was time
to break down through the cloud layer and land. Their watches
and clocks, however, told them this was impossible.

This placed them in a precarious position. If they believed
their instruments and came down through the cloud layer too
soon, they might be spotted by the enemy and shot down with anti-
aircraft fire. If they believed their clocks and came down too late,
they would overshoot the airfield and perish in the desert beyond.

They chose to ignore the instruments and believe their gut-
level hunch. They stayed up. They overshot the airfield and their
plane was found days later, crashed in the desert. All the crew-
men had perished.

The story of the *Lady Be Good* is a microcosm of life. We are all on the *Lady Be Good,* and we are all in flight. In making the determination on where and when to land we have to make decisions. And for those decisions we must choose whether we look outside ourselves . . . whether we trust our gut-level hunches or whether we look for an instrument panel.

The Bible offers itself as the source of truth. The Bible presents itself as the great, cosmic "instrument panel." It tells us where we came from, where we are, and where we are going. It is up to us to decide whether we accept the "readings" we get from it.

The Bible does not defend itself. It was written to people who accepted its message and therefore spends little time convincing its readers of its authenticity. Charles Spurgeon once said, "The Bible does not need to be defended any more than a caged lion needs to be defended. All we need to do is let it out of its cage, and it will defend itself."

The fundamental assertion that the Bible makes concerning itself is that, in spite of the human collaboration in the writing of it, the Bible is a revelation of God to man, it was written without error, and it can be trusted to reveal truth to us regarding God, man, life, and death.

As we begin our study of the doctrine of the Bible, we will adopt a pattern that will be followed throughout this section:

I. You will be asked to review the previous chapter.

II. You will then be given an overview of the doctrine, focusing on three things:

   A. The four major subdivisions of each doctrine, assigning a visual symbol to each.

   B. A brief definition for each subdivision, followed by an expansion.

   C. A central Scripture passage for each subdivision.

III. Three of the doctrines will require some additional attention, which will be dealt with under the heading, "Further Considerations."

I.   **Review:** Fill in the blanks. For answers, see pages 7–8.

Ten Great Doctrines of Systematic Theology

1. B_IBLE_

2. G_OD_

3. C_HRIST_

4. H_OLY_   S_PIRIT_

5. A_NGELS_

6. M_AN_

7. S_ALV._

8. S_IN_

9. C_HURCH_

10. F_UTURE_   T_HINGS_

II.   **The Four Major Subdivisions of the Doctrine of the Bible Are:**

1. Revelation

2. Inspiration

 3. Illumination

 4. Interpretation

(As you read the definitions of the doctrine subdivisions, notice the words in italics. Immediately following the definitions, they are repeated with blank spaces in place of the italic words. Fill in the blank spaces.)

SYMBOL:	SUBDIVISION:	DEFINITION:
	1. Revelation:	The Bible was *revealed* to man by God.
	Revelation:	The Bible was _____ to man by God.

God made known to man that which He wanted man to know. Some of the information related to present-day instruction on how to live and be rightly related to God and one's fellow man. Other information related to prophetic statements about the future. Hebrews 3:7 says, "Therefore, just as the Holy Spirit says. . . ." Then it quotes a passage from Psalms, which was written by King David, indicating that the human writing was *revealed* by God.

CENTRAL PASSAGE:

Therefore, just as the Holy Spirit says, "Today, if you hear His voice. . . ." (Hebrews 3:7)

SYMBOL*:	SUBDIVISION:	DEFINITION:

2. Inspiration: God saw to it that when men wrote down His revelation, they did so *without error.*

Inspiration: God saw to it that when men wrote down His revelation, they did so _____.

Not all of God's revelation to man was recorded in the Bible. Some of it was very personal, between God and one individual. But for that part of God's revelation to man that was written down, God became involved in the recording process to such a degree that, while He did not dictate or override each individual author's personality, He saw to it that what the writer did record was what He wanted recorded and that it was *without error.*

CENTRAL PASSAGE:

Men moved by the Holy Spirit spoke from God. (2 Peter 1:21)

SYMBOL:	SUBDIVISION:	DEFINITION:

3. Illumination: The Holy Spirit must enable people to *understand* and *embrace* the truth of Scripture.

Illumination: The Holy Spirit must enable people to _____ and _____ the truth of Scripture.

Man's natural ability to grasp and embrace the information in the Bible is limited. Much of it is spiritual information that man does not readily understand or accept. To overcome this fact,

---

* This symbol was chosen because the central passage says holy men of old were borne along by the Holy Spirit (symbolized by the dove) as they recorded God's revelation.

the Holy Spirit gradually illumines the receptive mind to *understand* and *embrace* more and more of the Bible, as the Christian matures in his or her spiritual walk.

CENTRAL PASSAGE:

Now we have received, not the spirit of the world, but the Spirit who is from God, that we might know the things freely given to us by God. (1 Corinthians 2:12)

SYMBOL:	SUBDIVISION:	DEFINITION:

4. Interpretation: We must be diligent *students* of Scripture to understand its deeper teachings.

Interpretation: We must be diligent _____ of Scripture to understand its deeper teachings.

Gaining a deeper grasp of the Bible is a two-way street. It is true that it will not happen unless the Holy Spirit illumines the mind of the Christian, but neither will it happen unless the Christian is diligent in pursuing biblical knowledge. The more the Christian reads and studies the Bible, the more the Holy Spirit will illumine his or her mind, which encourages the *student* to read and study further.

CENTRAL PASSAGE:

Be diligent to present yourself approved to God as a workman who does not need to be ashamed, handling accurately the word of truth. (2 Timothy 2:15)

The Doctrine of the Bible

(Write the titles of the four subdivisions on the lines below.)

SYMBOL:	**SUBDIVISION:**	**DEFINITION:**

1. R_eveLATion_   The Bible was *revealed* to man by God.

CENTRAL PASSAGE: Hebrews 3:7

SYMBOL:	**SUBDIVISION:**	**DEFINITION:**

2. I_nspiration_   God saw to it that when men wrote down His revelation, they did so *without error.*

CENTRAL PASSAGE: 2 Peter 1:21

SYMBOL:	**SUBDIVISION:**	**DEFINITION:**

3. I_llumination_   The Holy Spirit must enable people to *understand* and *embrace* the truth of Scripture.

CENTRAL PASSAGE: 1 Corinthians 2:12

SYMBOL:	**SUBDIVISION:**	**DEFINITION:**

4. I_nterpretation_   We must be diligent *students* of the Scripture to understand its deeper teachings.

CENTRAL PASSAGE: 2 Timothy 2:15

The Doctrine of the Bible

(Name the four subdivisions of the Doctrine of the Bible, and fill in the key words in the definitions.)

SYMBOL: **SUBDIVISION:**   **DEFINITION:**

1. _____   The Bible was _____ ____ to man by God.

CENTRAL PASSAGE: Hebrews 3:7

SYMBOL: **SUBDIVISION:**   **DEFINITION:**

2. _____   God saw to it that when men wrote down His revelation, they did so _____.

CENTRAL PASSAGE: 2 Peter 1:21

SYMBOL: **SUBDIVISION:**   **DEFINITION:**

3. _____   The Holy Spirit must enable people to _____ and _____ the truth of Scripture.

CENTRAL PASSAGE: 1 Corinthians 2:12

SYMBOL: **SUBDIVISION:**   **DEFINITION:**

4. _____   We must be diligent _____ of Scripture to understand its deeper teachings.

CENTRAL PASSAGE: 2 Timothy 2:15

Self-Test

(Fill in the blanks.)

1. R_____ The Bible was _____ to man by God.
2. I_____ God saw to it that when men wrote down His revelation, they did so _____.
3. I_____ The Holy Spirit must enable people to _____ and _____ the truth of Scripture.
4. I_____ We must be diligent _____ of Scripture to understand its deeper teachings.

Ten Great Doctrines of Systematic Theology

(From memory, fill in the name of doctrine number one. See the Appendix for the answer.)

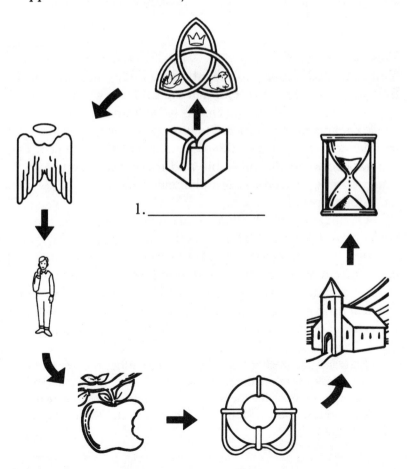

1._____

THE DOCTRINE OF GOD

God is not to be found in the laboratory. He cannot be proved. But then, love is not to be found in the laboratory. Neither is courage, nor longing, nor hope. God is to be found in the courtroom. While data cannot be garnered to prove His existence, evidence can be amassed to demonstrate the probability of His existence. There *is* a gap between the probable and the proved. But then, few things can be proved to the unbelieving mind. Unbelief never has enough proof.

C. S. Lewis, the brilliant Christian scholar who taught at both Cambridge and Oxford, readily admitted his reluctance to accept the existence of God. Yet he kept an open mind in the investigation of the evidence and found himself being convinced in spite of himself. He wrote in his book *Surprised by Joy* that he was teaching at Magdalen College at the University of Oxford when he had an encounter with an atheist intellectual:

> Early in 1926 the hardest boiled of all the atheists I ever knew sat in my room on the other side of the fire and remarked that the evidence for the historicity of the Gospels was really surprisingly good. "Rum thing," he went on. "Rum thing. It

almost looks as if it had really happened once." To understand the shattering impact of it, you would need to know the man (who has certainly never since shown any interest in Christianity). If he, the cynic of cynics, the toughest of the toughs, were not—as I would still have put it—"safe," where could I turn? Was there then no escape?

You must picture me alone in that room at Magdalen, night after night, feeling, whenever my mind lifted even for a second from my work, the steady, unrelenting hand of Him whom I so earnestly desired not to meet. That which I greatly feared had at last come upon me. In the Trinity Term of 1929 I gave in, and admitted that God was God, and knelt and prayed: perhaps, that night, the most dejected and reluctant convert in all England. I did not then see what is now the most shining and obvious thing: the Divine humility which will accept a convert even on such terms. The Prodigal Son at least walked home on his own feet. But who can duly adore the Love which will open the high gates to a prodigal who is brought in kicking, struggling, resentful, and darting his eyes in every direction for a chance of escape?

If you look for God in the laboratory, you will not find Him. If you look for Him in the courtroom, the amount of evidence can be very satisfying—enough to give a reasonable doubt about a universe without Him and make it reasonable to believe in Him.

I.   Review: Fill in the blanks.

The Doctrine of the Bible

1. R _____

2. I _____

3. I _____

4. I _____

II. The Four Major Subdivisions of the Doctrine of God Are:

 1. Existence

 2. Attributes

 3. Sovereignty

 4. Trinity

(As you read the definitions of the doctrine subdivisions, notice the words in italics. Immediately following the definitions, they are repeated with blank spaces in place of the italic words. Fill in the blank spaces.)

SYMBOL:	SUBDIVISION:	DEFINITION:

1. Existence: God *exists.*

Existence: God _____.

In a scientific culture, some are reluctant to believe in a being they cannot see, hear, smell, taste, or touch. However, God cannot be dealt with in the laboratory. He must be dealt with in the courtroom. It is impossible to generate *proof* of His existence, so we must look for *evidence* of His existence. While the Bible simply assumes that God *exists,* it also provides excellent evidence, so that believing in His existence is an intellectually reasonable thing to do.

CENTRAL PASSAGE:

For since the creation of the world His invisible attributes, His eternal power and divine nature, have been clearly seen, being understood through what has been made. (Romans 1:20)

SYMBOL:	**SUBDIVISION:**	**DEFINITION:**

2. Attributes: The fundamental *characteristics* of God.

Attributes: The fundamental _____ of God.

God is a personal being, and as such has individual *characteristics* that distinguish Him from all other beings. These characteristics are called "attributes." Some of His attributes are shared by mankind since God created man after His personal image. These are called "personal" attributes. He has other characteristics, however, which go beyond man and are true of Him alone. These are the attributes that define "deity" and are called "divine" attributes. We will look more closely at them later.

CENTRAL PASSAGE:

Selected passages to be seen later.

SYMBOL: **SUBDIVISION:**   **DEFINITION:**

3. Sovereignty: God can do whatever He *wills.*

Sovereignty: God can do whatever He _____.

God is all powerful and has the ability to do whatever He wills. This sovereignty is only exercised in harmony with His goodness, righteousness, and other attributes, and it extends to the entirety of creation for all time. In His sovereignty, He has determined everything that has happened and will happen, and yet has done so in such a way that man has true "volition," or choice. This is one of the mysteries, or "unexplainable" things, of Scripture.

CENTRAL PASSAGE:

For I know that the LORD is great,
And that our LORD is above all gods.
Whatever the LORD pleases, He does,
In heaven and in earth, in the seas and in all
    the deeps. (Psalm 135:5–6)

SYMBOL: **SUBDIVISION:**   **DEFINITION:**

4. Trinity: God is *three* persons, yet *one.*

Trinity: God is _____ persons, yet _____.

Another mystery of the Scripture is the Trinity. The Bible says distinctly that there is only one true God (Deuteronomy 6:4). But it also seems to say with equal clarity that there was a man, Jesus Christ, who claimed equality with God the Father, and there is someone called the Holy Spirit who is also equal with God the Father. How do you put that together? Historically, the concept has been termed the

"Trinity." There is *one* God who exists in *three* persons. While it is impossible to give an illustration of the Trinity, the evidence remains and has been embraced as a fundamental teaching of Christianity from the beginning.

CENTRAL PASSAGES:

Hear, O Israel! The LORD is our God, the LORD is one! (Deuteronomy 6:4)

The grace of the Lord Jesus Christ, and the love of God, and the fellowship of the Holy Spirit, be with you all. (2 Corinthians 13:14)

The Doctrine of God

(Write the titles of the four subdivisions on the lines below.)

SYMBOL:	SUBDIVISION:	DEFINITION:

1. E_____ God *exists.*

CENTRAL PASSAGE: Romans 1:20

SYMBOL:	SUBDIVISION:	DEFINITION:

2. A _____ The fundamental *characteristics* of God.

CENTRAL PASSAGE: Selected passages. (see pages 27–28)

| SYMBOL: | SUBDIVISION: | DEFINITION: |

3. S_____ God can do whatever He *wills*.

CENTRAL PASSAGE: Psalm 135:5–6

| SYMBOL: | SUBDIVISION: | DEFINITION: |

4. T_____ God is *three* persons, yet *one*.

CENTRAL PASSAGES: Deuteronomy 6:4
2 Corinthians 13:14

The Doctrine of God

(Name the four subdivisions of the Doctrine of God, and fill in the key words in the definitions.)

| SYMBOL: | SUBDIVISION: | DEFINITION: |

1. _____ God _____.

CENTRAL PASSAGE: Romans 1:20

| SYMBOL: | SUBDIVISION: | DEFINITION: |

2. _____ The fundamental _____ of God.

CENTRAL PASSAGE: Selected passages. (see pages 27–28)

SYMBOL:	SUBDIVISION:	DEFINITION:

3. _____ God can do whatever He
_____ .

CENTRAL PASSAGE: Psalm 135:5–6

SYMBOL:	SUBDIVISION:	DEFINITION:

4. _____ God is _____ persons, yet
_____ .

CENTRAL PASSAGES: Deuteronomy 6:4
2 Corinthians 13:14

Self-Test

(Fill in the blanks.)

1. E_____ God _____ .
2. A_____ The fundamental _____ of God.
3. S_____ God can do whatever He _____ .
4. T_____ God is _____ persons, yet _____ .

III. Further Consideration of the Attributes of God

The attributes of God require further consideration. While God has many attributes, or characteristics, we will focus on six primary attributes. Three are divine attributes, and three are personal attributes.

A. Divine Attributes

1. Omnipotence: God is all *powerful*.

CENTRAL PASSAGE:

I know that Thou canst do all things,
And that no purpose of Thine can be thwarted. (Job 42:2 KJV)

2. Omnipresence: God is *present* everywhere simultaneously.

CENTRAL PASSAGE:

If I ascend to heaven, Thou art there;
If I make my bed in Sheol, behold, Thou
art there. (Psalm 139:8 KJV)

3. Omniscience: God *knows* all things.

CENTRAL PASSAGE:

Even before there is a word on my tongue,
Behold, O LORD, Thou dost know it all.
(Psalm 139:4 KJV)

Review: Divine Attributes

1. Omnipotence: God is all _____. (Job 42:2)

2. Omnipresence: God is _____ everywhere simultaneously. (Psalm 139:8)

3. Omniscience: God _____ all things. (Psalm 139:4)

B. **Personal Attributes**

1. Holy: God is *without evil* and is only good.

   CENTRAL PASSAGE: Isaiah 5:16

2. Love: God seeks the *best* for *others.*

   CENTRAL PASSAGE: 1 John 4:8

3. Just: God applies righteous *consequences* equally
   to everyone.

   CENTRAL PASSAGE: Psalm 19:9

Review: Personal Attributes

1. Holy: God is _____ and is only good.
   (Isaiah 5:16)

2. Love: God seeks the _____ for _____.
   (1 John 4:8)

3. Just: God applies righteous _____ equally
   to everyone. (Psalm 19:9)

Self-Test

A. Match the six attributes of God with their definitions by writing the correct letter in the blank.

Omnipotence _____

Omnipresence _____

Omniscience _____

Holy _____

Love _____

Just _____

A. God seeks the *best* for *others.*

B. God applies righteous *consequences* equally to everyone.

C. God is *without evil* and is only good.

D. God is *present* everywhere simultaneously.

E. God *knows* all things.

F. God is all *powerful.*

B. Fill in the blanks.

God's three divine attributes are:

1. _____

2. _____

3. _____

God's three personal attributes are:

1. _____

2. _____

3. _____

It is worth repeating that there are many more characteristics of God than these. These six were chosen because they were among the most striking and well-known attributes.

Ten Great Doctrines of Systematic Theology

(From memory, fill in the names of doctrines one and two. See the Appendix for answers.)

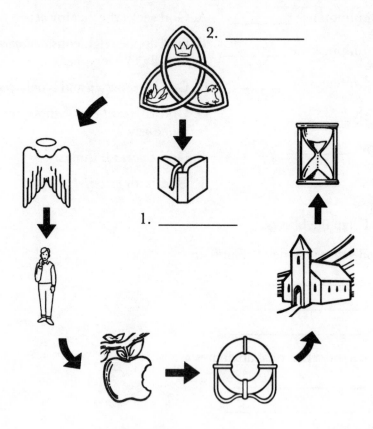

2. _____

1. _____

THREE

THE DOCTRINE OF CHRIST

Attitudes about Jesus are varied and often are strongly held. From denying that a person named Jesus of Nazareth ever existed to believing that He was God incarnate, people demonstrate their conviction about Him by ignoring Him or worshiping Him.

Perhaps the most popular concept of Jesus is that, while He was not divine, He was a great moral teacher and leader. While He is no more God than you or I, He is a wonderful example to follow.

This is a difficult concept to hold consistently. The reason is expressed skillfully by C. S. Lewis, who wrote in his book *Mere Christianity:*

> That is the thing we must not say. A man who was merely a man and said the sort of things that Jesus said would not be a great moral teacher. He would either be a lunatic on the level of a man who says he is a poached egg—or else he would be the devil of hell. You must make your choice. Either this man was, and is, the son of God; or else a madman or something worse. You can shut Him up for a fool, you can spit at Him and kill Him as a demon; or you can fall at His feet and call Him Lord and God. But let us not come with any patronizing nonsense about His being a great human teacher. He has not left that open to us. He did not intend to.

The position of the Bible is straightforward in presenting Jesus as divine, the Son of God, the second person of the Trinity. He is fully man and fully God. If He were not man, He could not have died for our sins, and if He were not God, His death would have accomplished nothing.

To understand the Bible's position on Jesus, it must be grasped that Jesus is presented as the Messiah, the Savior of the world who was prophesied throughout the Old Testament, who would come to die for the sins of the world and who would come again to establish righteousness in a new heaven and new earth.

I.   Review: Fill in the blanks.

The Doctrine of the Bible

    1. R_____

    2. I_____

    3. I_____

    4. I_____

The Doctrine of God

    1. E_____

    2. A_____

    3. S_____

    4. T_____

II. The Four Major Subdivisions of the Doctrine of Christ Are:

1. Deity

 2. Humanity

 3. Resurrection

 4. Return

(As you read the definitions of the doctrine subdivisions, notice the words in italics. Immediately following the definitions, they are repeated with blank spaces in place of the italic words. Fill in the blank spaces.)

SYMBOL:	**SUBDIVISION:**	**DEFINITION:**

1. Deity: Jesus of Nazareth was *God* incarnate.

Deity: Jesus of Nazareth was _____ incarnate.

Though Jesus was man, He was also *God*. The second member of the Trinity existed before He was born as Jesus of Nazareth. Christ was active in the creation of the world and during the Old Testament. When the timing was right, the Christ, the second person of the Trinity, became incarnate as Jesus of Nazareth but did not forfeit His divinity at any time.

CENTRAL PASSAGE:

In the beginning was the Word, and the Word was with God, and the Word was God. (John 1:1)

SYMBOL: **SUBDIVISION:**   **DEFINITION:**

2. Humanity: Christ was a *man,* Jesus of Nazareth.

Humanity: Christ was a _____, Jesus of Nazareth.

Though Jesus was God, He was also *man.* Christ took on the form of humanity, and though He did not sin He tasted all other human experiences, including hunger, fatigue, and sorrow, etc. He was supernaturally conceived, was born of a virgin, and lived a fairly normal early life as a carpenter's son in Nazareth of Galilee. As a man, He was crucified, died, and was buried.

CENTRAL PASSAGE:

And the Word became flesh, and dwelt among us, and we beheld His glory, glory as of the only begotten from the Father, full of grace and truth. (John 1:14)

SYMBOL: **SUBDIVISION:**   **DEFINITION:**

3. Resurrection: After being killed, Jesus was *raised* to life again.

Resurrection: After being killed, Jesus was _____ to life again.

After being falsely accused and tried in a series of kangaroo courts, Jesus was subjected to the form of capital punishment reserved for non-Roman citizens. He was flogged, a savage punishment which, itself, killed 60 percent of its victims; then He was nailed to a wooden cross where He died. Afterward, He was wrapped in burial clothes and placed in a sealed tomb where He remained for three days. At the end of that time, a miraculous earthquake moved the stone from the mouth of the tomb to reveal that Jesus was *raised* from the dead after three days, just as He said He would be.

CENTRAL PASSAGE:

Who was declared the Son of God with power by the resurrection from the dead, according to the Spirit of holiness, Jesus Christ our Lord. (Romans 1:4)

SYMBOL: **SUBDIVISION:** **DEFINITION:**

4. Return: Jesus will *return* to earth at some time in the future.

Return: Jesus will _____ to earth at some time in the future.

The picture of the Messiah in the Old Testament was an uncertain one. Some of the prophetic passages spoke of a humble-servant Messiah while other passages spoke of a glorious and powerful king. So stark was the contrast between these two kinds of passages that some Old Testament scholars thought there would be two Messiahs. With the additional revelation in the New Testament, we now know how to reconcile these passages. Jesus came the first time as a humble servant and died for the sins of mankind. After He was resurrected, He ascended into heaven to sit at the right hand of God the Father. Some day in the future, and according to Biblical prophecy it could be soon, Jesus will *return* to earth as a powerful and glorious king to institute righteousness on the earth.

CENTRAL PASSAGE:

Looking for the blessed hope and the appearing of the glory of our great God and Savior, Christ Jesus. (Titus 2:13)

The Doctrine of Christ

(Write the titles of the four subdivisions on the lines below.)

SYMBOL: **SUBDIVISION:**   **DEFINITION:**

1. D_____   Jesus of Nazareth was *God* incarnate.

CENTRAL PASSAGE: John 1:1

SYMBOL: **SUBDIVISION:**   **DEFINITION:**

2. H_____   Christ was a *man*, Jesus of Nazareth.

CENTRAL PASSAGE: John 1:14

SYMBOL: **SUBDIVISION:**   **DEFINITION:**

3. R_____   After being killed, Jesus was *raised* to life again.

CENTRAL PASSAGE: Romans 1:4

SYMBOL: **SUBDIVISION:**   **DEFINITION:**

4. R_____   Jesus will *return* to earth at some time in the future.

CENTRAL PASSAGE: Titus 2:13

The Doctrine of Christ

(Name the four subdivisions of the Doctrine of Christ and fill in the key words in the definitions.)

SYMBOL: **SUBDIVISION:**   **DEFINITION:**

1. _____   Jesus of Nazareth was _____ incarnate.

CENTRAL PASSAGE: John 1:1

SYMBOL: **SUBDIVISION:**   **DEFINITION:**

2. _____   Christ was a _____, Jesus of Nazareth.

CENTRAL PASSAGE: John 1:14

SYMBOL: **SUBDIVISION:**   **DEFINITION:**

3. _____   After being killed, Jesus was _____ to life again.

CENTRAL PASSAGE: Romans 1:4

SYMBOL: **SUBDIVISION:**   **DEFINITION:**

4. _____   Jesus will _____ to earth at
                    some time in the future.

CENTRAL PASSAGE: Titus 2:13

Self-Test

(Fill in the blanks.)

1. D_____   Jesus of Nazareth was _____ incarnate.

2. H_____   Christ was a _____, Jesus of Nazareth.

3. R_____   After being killed, Jesus was _____ to life
                   again.

4. R_____   Jesus will _____ to earth at some time in
                                the future.

Ten Great Doctrines of Systematic Theology

(From memory, fill in the names of doctrines one through three. See the Appendix for answers.)

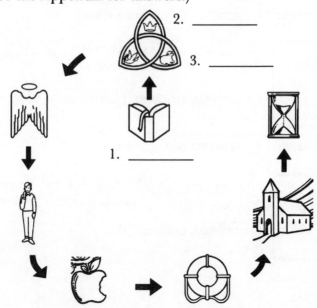

THE DOCTRINE OF
THE HOLY SPIRIT

The IRS has a "Conscience Fund" that receives anonymous contributions from people who have cheated the government out of money in the past and who want to make up for it to clear their conscience but don't want to risk criminal prosecution. The Conscience Fund received a check from a man who included the following note:

> I have not been able to sleep ever since I cheated you out of some money, so here is a check for $500. If I still can't sleep, I'll send you the rest.

In another example, a salesman called on a successful contractor with a bid for the materials for a large job the contractor was about to begin. He was invited into the contractor's office where they chatted for a moment before a secretary came and summoned the contractor into another office. Alone, the salesman noticed that there was a bid from a competitor's firm on the contractor's desk with all the numbers written clearly. The total amount of the bid was hidden, however, covered by a small orange juice can. Unable to contain his curiosity, the salesman picked up the orange juice can. When he did, thousands of BB's came pouring from the bottom of the can which had been cut out, flooded over the surface of the desk, and rained down on the floor. Without saying a word, the salesman turned, walked out of the office, and never returned.

We laugh at the first story and cringe at the second, because we see ourselves in both of them. We all have shortcomings and weakness. We all want to be more than we are. But we need help. Sometimes we need information. Sometimes we need assistance. Sometimes, we need to be challenged or confronted to change. This is a primary role of the Holy Spirit . . . to work with us in a mystical sort of way to become Christians and then to grow as Christians. He transforms us from what we were like in the past to what we should be like in the future. He is a friend, indeed, because He knows all about us and loves us anyway. He commits Himself to us to help us change . . . to be the sort of man or woman we long to be deep down in our souls.

I. Review: Fill in the blanks.

The Doctrine of the Bible

1. R_____

2. I_____

3. I_____

4. I_____

The Doctrine of God

1. E_____

2. A_____

3. S_____

4. T_____

The Doctrine of Christ

1. D_____

2. H_____

3. R_____

4. R_____

II. The Four Major Subdivisions of the Doctrine of the Holy Spirit Are:

 1. Personality

 2. Deity

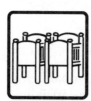 3. Salvation

 4. Gifts

(As you read the definitions of the doctrine subdivisions, notice the words in italics. Immediately following the definitions, they are repeated with blank spaces in place of the italic words. Fill in the blank spaces.)

SYMBOL: **SUBDIVISION:**   **DEFINITION:**

1. Personality: The Holy Spirit is a *personal* being, not an impersonal force.

Personality: The Holy Spirit is a _____ being, not an impersonal force.

The Holy Spirit is sometimes perceived as the religious equivalent of school spirit. This is not accurate. In the Bible, the Holy Spirit is treated as a person and given the attributes of *personality*, such as emotions, actions, intellect, and relationships.

CENTRAL PASSAGE:

And do not grieve the Holy Spirit of God, by whom you were sealed for the day of redemption. (Ephesians 4:30)

SYMBOL:	SUBDIVISION:	DEFINITION:

2. Deity: The Holy Spirit is *divine*, the third person of the Trinity.

Deity: The Holy Spirit is _____, the third person of the Trinity.

Not only is the Holy Spirit a personal being, He is also *divine*. He possesses divine attributes, such as omnipresence and omnipotence. He performed miracles only God could do, such as the creation of the world and the miraculous conception of Jesus. In addition, He is associated on an equal plane with the other members of the Trinity.

CENTRAL PASSAGE:

The grace of the Lord Jesus Christ, and the love of God, and the fellowship of the Holy Spirit, be with you all. (2 Corinthians 13:14)

SYMBOL:	SUBDIVISION:	DEFINITION:

3. Salvation: The Holy Spirit is *instrumental* in personal salvation.

Salvation: The Holy Spirit is _____ in personal salvation.

The Holy Spirit plays the *instrumental* role in the personal salvation of individuals who become Christians. It is the Holy Spirit who enables us to see our sinfulness and realize that we should turn from sin. It is the Holy Spirit who helps us see that, in order to become Christians, we must believe in Jesus, ask Him to forgive us of our sins and give us eternal life, and commit our lives to living for Him.

CENTRAL PASSAGE:

Selected passages to be seen later.

(Note: The significance of the two baby cribs lies in an acrostic. There are five primary areas of involvement by the Holy Spirit in personal salvation: conviction, regeneration, indwelling, baptism, and sealing. The first letters from each of these words spells "CRIBS." We will study the CRIBS concept in more detail later.)

SYMBOL:	**SUBDIVISION:**	**DEFINITION:**

4. Gifts: The Holy Spirit imparts *spiritual* abilities to Christians.

Gifts: The Holy Spirit imparts _____ abilities to Christians.

God wants to use each of us to minister to others. The Holy Spirit gives us a special *spiritual* "gift" to minister to others. It is something we enjoy doing and something at which we are effective. However, since God is working through us with this gift, the results must always be attributed to Him and not to ourselves. We must guard against two imbalances. We must not become discouraged if our results are meager, and we must not become inflated if our results are abundant. For in the true exercise of spiritual gifts, it is God who produces the results, whether meager or abundant.

CENTRAL PASSAGE:

Now there are varieties of gifts, but the same Spirit. . . . But one and the same Spirit works all these things distributing to each one individually just as He wills. (1 Corinthians 12:4, 11)

The Doctrine of the Holy Spirit

(Write the titles of the four subdivisions on the lines below.)

SYMBOL: **SUBDIVISION:**   **DEFINITION:**

1. P_____   The Holy Spirit is a *personal* being, not an impersonal force.

CENTRAL PASSAGE: Ephesians 4:30

SYMBOL: **SUBDIVISION:**   **DEFINITION:**

2. D_____   The Holy Spirit is *divine*, the third person of the Trinity.

CENTRAL PASSAGE: 2 Corinthians 13:14

SYMBOL: **SUBDIVISION:**   **DEFINITION:**

3. S_____   The Holy Spirit is *instrumental* in personal salvation.

CENTRAL PASSAGE: Selected passages. (see pages 46–48)

SYMBOL: **SUBDIVISION:**   **DEFINITION:**

4. G_____   The Holy Spirit imparts *spiritual* abilities to Christians.

CENTRAL PASSAGE: 1 Corinthians 12:4, 11

The Doctrine of the Holy Spirit

(Name the four subdivisions of the Doctrine of the Holy Spirit and fill in the key words in the definitions.)

SYMBOL: **SUBDIVISION:**   **DEFINITION:**

1. _____   The Holy Spirit is a _____ being, not an impersonal force.

CENTRAL PASSAGE: Ephesians 4:30

SYMBOL: **SUBDIVISION:**   **DEFINITION:**

2. _____   The Holy Spirit is _____, the third person of the Trinity.

CENTRAL PASSAGE: 2 Corinthians 13:14

SYMBOL: **SUBDIVISION:**   **DEFINITION:**

3. _____   The Holy Spirit is _____ in personal salvation.

CENTRAL PASSAGE: Selected passages. (see pages 46–48)

SYMBOL: SUBDIVISION: DEFINITION:

4. _____   The Holy Spirit imparts _____
                     abilities to Christians.

CENTRAL PASSAGE: 1 Corinthians 12:4, 11

Self-Test

(Fill in the blanks.)

1. P_____   The Holy Spirit is _____ being, not an
                  impersonal force.

2. D_____   The Holy Spirit is _____, the third person
                  of the Trinity.

3. S_____   The Holy Spirit is _____ in personal
                  salvation.

4. G_____   The Holy Spirit imparts _____ abilities
                  to Christians.

III. Further Consideration of the Holy Spirit's Work in Salvation

The work of the Holy Spirit in personal salvation requires further consideration. There are five primary areas of involvement.

1. Conviction: Revealing a *need* to *change.*

                  The Holy Spirit convinces a person of his or her *need* to *change* some thought, attitude, or action. This phenomenon is sometimes accompanied by an acute sense of guilt over wrongdoing.

                  CENTRAL PASSAGE:

                  And He [the Holy Spirit], when He comes, will convict the world concerning sin, and righteousness, and judgment. (John 16:8)

2. Regeneration: Imparting a new spirit and *eternal life* with God.

                  According to the Bible, everyone lives forever, either with God in heaven or separated from

Him in hell. When a person becomes a Christian, the Holy Spirit imparts to him or her a new spirit and *eternal life* with God in heaven.

CENTRAL PASSAGE:

He saved us, not on the basis of deeds which we have done in righteousness, but according to His mercy, by the washing of regeneration and renewing by the Holy Spirit. (Titus 3:5)

3. Indwelling:

Living *within* a believer.

The Holy Spirit mysteriously "takes up residence" *within* a person when the person becomes a believer, encouraging and strengthening him or her to live a proper lifestyle.

CENTRAL PASSAGE:

You are not in the flesh but in the Spirit, if indeed the Spirit of God lives in you. But if anyone does not have the Spirit of Christ, he does not belong to Him. (Romans 8:9)

4. Baptism:

Placing a believer, spiritually, in the Body of Christ.

The "Body of Christ" is a term given to the totality of all believers in Him. To *baptize* means to "place into." Technically, to be baptized into the Body of Christ means to be a member of that spiritual organism.

CENTRAL PASSAGE:

For by one Spirit we were all baptized into one body, whether Jews or Greeks, whether slaves or free, and we were all made to drink of one Spirit. (1 Corinthians 12:13)

5. Sealing:

Guaranteeing the believer's relationship to God.

The Holy Spirit becomes the *guarantee* of our spiritual inheritance, to be fully realized when we die. This means once a person has been regenerated, indwelt, and baptized into the Body of Christ, his or her position is secure, "sealed . . . with the Holy Spirit of promise" until the day of redemption. (Ephesians 1:13)

CENTRAL PASSAGE:

In Him [Christ] you also trusted, after you heard the word of truth, the gospel of your salvation: in whom also, having believed, you were sealed with the Holy Spirit of promise. (Ephesians 1:13–14 NKJV)

Self-Test

A. The five works of the Holy Spirit in personal salvation are:

1. C_____

2. R_____

3. I_____

4. B_____

5. S_____

B. Match the term with the definition by writing the correct letter in the blank.

Conviction_____

Regeneration_____

Indwelling_____

Baptism_____

Sealing_____

A. Imparting a new spirit and *eternal life* with God.

B. *Guaranteeing* the believer's relationship to God.

C. Revealing a *need* to *change*.

D. Living *within* a believer.

E. *Placing* a believer, spiritually, in the Body of Christ.

Ten Great Doctrines of Systematic Theology

(From memory, fill in the names of doctrines one through four. See the Appendix for answers.)

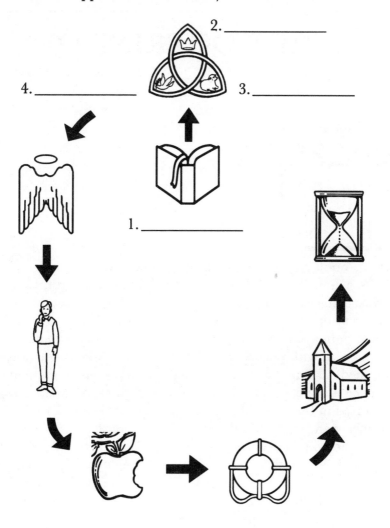

FIVE

THE DOCTRINE OF ANGELS

In his book entitled *Angels,* Billy Graham tells the story of Dr. S. W. Mitchell, a well-known Philadelphia neurologist, who was awakened from sleep one rainy night by a little girl, poorly dressed and very upset. She said her mother was very sick, and would he come right away. He followed the girl and found the mother desperately ill with pneumonia. After attending her and arranging for medical care, he complimented the sick woman on the intelligence and persistence of her little daughter. As *Reader's Digest* reported in the original story, the woman looked at Dr. Mitchell strangely and said, "My daughter died a month ago." She added, "Her shoes and coat are in the clothes closet there." Puzzled, Dr. Mitchell went to the closet and opened the door. There hung the very coat worn by the little girl who had brought him to care for her mother. It was warm and dry and could not possibly have been out in the inclement weather.

Might the "little girl" have been an angel, sent to aid the stricken mother?

Mr. Graham also tells the story of John G. Paton, a missionary in the New Hebrides Islands. One evening, natives surrounded the missionary compound with the intent of burning down the compound and killing Mr. Paton and his wife. The missionaries prayed fervently all night and were surprised and relieved to witness the natives leaving the next morning.

A year later, the chief of the hostile tribe was converted to Christianity. He told the Patons that he and his tribe had fully intended to destroy the compound and kill the Patons that fateful night a year ago but had been stopped by the army of men surrounding the compound. "Who were all those men you had with you there?" the chief asked. "There were no men there; just my wife and I," replied Mr. Paton. The chief argued that they had seen many men standing guard—hundreds of big men in shining garments with drawn swords in their hands. They seemed to circle the mission station so that the natives were afraid to attack.

Again, angels?

When the brilliant scholar Mortimer Adler undertook to edit *Great Books of the Western World* for the Encyclopedia Britannica Company, he included "Angels" as one of the great themes. Personally curious, Mr. Adler went on to write a book on angels, and in doing so, discovered that from before Aristotle's time to the present day, scholars and philosophers have taken angels seriously.

It is difficult to prove the existence and work of angels. They are not usually perceived by our five senses and are therefore not subject to scientific scrutiny. Nevertheless, they are found throughout the Bible, interwoven into many of the major events of Scripture.

I. Review: Fill in the blanks.

The Doctrine of the Bible

1. R_____

2. I_____

3. I_____

4. I_____

The Doctrine of God

1. E_____

2. A_____

3. S_____

4. T_____

The Doctrine of Christ

1. D_____

2. H_____

3. R_____

4. R_____

The Doctrine of the Holy Spirit

1. P_____

2. D_____

3. S_____

4. G_____

II. The Four Major Subdivisions of the Doctrine of Angels Are:

 1. Angels

 2. Demons

 3. Satan

 4. Defenses

(As you read the definitions of the doctrine subdivisions, notice the words in italics. Immediately following the definitions, they are repeated with blank spaces in place of the italic words. Fill in the blank spaces.)

SYMBOL: **SUBDIVISION:** **DEFINITION:**

1. Angels: Ministering *spirits* from God.

Angels: Ministering _____ from God.

The Bible teaches that God uses a numberless army of angels to help execute His will in heaven and earth, and that among their duties is ministering to Christians. Perhaps this is where the concept of guardian angels came from. They are personal beings, *spirits* that God created before Adam and Eve, and are not "ghosts" of people who have died.

CENTRAL PASSAGE:

Are they [angels] not all ministering spirits, sent out to render service for the sake of those who will inherit salvation? (Hebrews 1:14)

SYMBOL: **SUBDIVISION:** **DEFINITION:**

2. Demons: Angels who *fell.*

Demons: Angels who _____.

The Bible teaches that a large number of the "righteous angels" rebelled against God and now form an evil army under the command of the devil, who uses them to further his will, which is counter to the will of God. This corruption is often referred to as the *"fall"* of these angels.

CENTRAL PASSAGE:

And the angels who did not keep their proper domain, but left their own abode, He has reserved in everlasting chains under darkness for the judgment of the great day. (Jude 6 NKJV)

SYMBOL:	SUBDIVISION:	DEFINITION:

3. Satan: The highest angel who *fell*.

Satan: The highest angel who _____.

The Bible teaches that Satan was originally the highest angel, but because of pride he *fell*, rebelling against God and leading many lesser angels to rebel against Him also. In doing this he became evil and corrupt. He is a real entity who oversees the forces of darkness in the world and seeks to neutralize and overthrow the will of God.

CENTRAL PASSAGE:

Be sober, be vigilant; because your adversary the devil walks about like a roaring lion, seeking whom he may devour. (1 Peter 5:8 NKJV)

SYMBOL:	SUBDIVISION:	DEFINITION:

4. Defenses: Using God's *protection*.

Defenses: Using God's _____.

In the Bible, Satan is called the *deceiver* and the *destroyer*. He deceives in order to destroy. A primary strategy is to make that which is wrong look right and that which is right look wrong. The Bible teaches that *protection* from Satan is available to the Christian. These spiritual defenses will be dealt with in greater detail later.

CENTRAL PASSAGE:

Selected passages to be seen later.

The Doctrine of Angels

(Write the titles of the four subdivisions on the lines below.)

SYMBOL: **SUBDIVISION:**   **DEFINITION:**

1. A_____   Ministering *spirits* from God.

CENTRAL PASSAGE: Hebrews 1:14

SYMBOL: **SUBDIVISION:**   **DEFINITION:**

2. D_____   Angels who *fell*.

CENTRAL PASSAGE: Jude 6

SYMBOL: **SUBDIVISION:**   **DEFINITION:**

3. S_____   The highest angel who *fell*.

CENTRAL PASSAGE: 1 Peter 5:8

SYMBOL: **SUBDIVISION:**   **DEFINITION:**

4. D_____   Using God's *protection*.

CENTRAL PASSAGE: Selected passages.
(see page 57)

The Doctrine of Angels
(Name the four subdivisions of the Doctrine of
Angels and fill in the key words in the definitions.)

SYMBOL:	**SUBDIVISION:**	**DEFINITION:**

1. _____   Ministering _____ from
                 God.

CENTRAL PASSAGE: Hebrews 1:14

SYMBOL:	**SUBDIVISION:**	**DEFINITION:**

2. _____   Angels who _____.

CENTRAL PASSAGE: Jude 6

SYMBOL:	**SUBDIVISION:**	**DEFINITION:**

3. _____   The highest angel who _____.

CENTRAL PASSAGE: 1 Peter 5:8

SYMBOL:	**SUBDIVISION:**	**DEFINITION:**

4. _____   Using God's _____.

CENTRAL PASSAGE: Selected passages.
                    (see page 57)

Self-Test

(Fill in the blanks.)

1. A_____   Ministering _____ from God.

2. D_____   Angels who _____.

3. S_____   The highest angel who _____.

4. D_____   Using God's _____.

III. Further Consideration of the Believer's Defenses

The believer's defenses against the efforts of Satan to deceive and destroy him or her require further consideration. There are three primary facets to the believer's defense system.

1. Alertness:

The Christian must know Satan's intention and be *alert* to his advances.

CENTRAL PASSAGE:

Be sober, be vigilant; because your adversary the devil walks about like a roaring lion, seeking whom he may devour. (1 Peter 5:8 NKJV)

2. Armor:

The Christian has defenses that are metaphorically called *armor*, which protect him or her from Satan's devices.

CENTRAL PASSAGE:

Therefore, take up the whole armor of God, that you may be able to withstand in the evil day, and having done all, to stand. (Ephesians 6:13 NKJV)

3. Resistance:

Once the Christian is aware of Satan's intentions and is using the "spiritual armor" discussed in Ephesians 6, he or she may *resist* any suspected Satanic advances with confidence of victory.

CENTRAL PASSAGE:

Therefore submit to God. Resist the devil and he will flee from you. (James 4:7 NKJV)

Self-Test

A. The believer's defenses are:

1. A_____

2. A_____

3. R_____

Ten Great Doctrines of Systematic Theology

(From memory, fill in the names of doctrines one through five. See the Appendix for answers.)

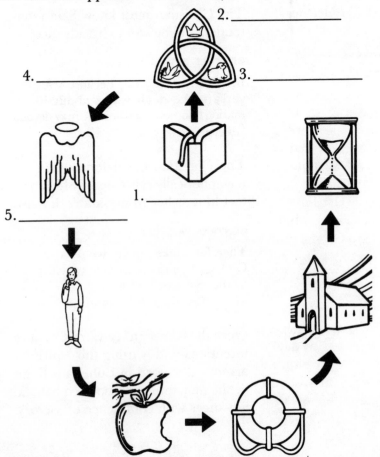

THE DOCTRINE OF MAN

If the full power of the human mind were manifested by an individual, the world would assume that person was a god. The power of the brain is beyond comprehension. Scientists estimate that the most brilliant among us use perhaps 10 percent of its capacity. Yet that might be wildly overstated when we ponder glimpses of its potential.

Mozart wrote his first full-length orchestral piece when he was only eight years old. Amazing as that is, it pales in comparison with other possibilities.

One of the most arresting speculations arises from an observation of people suffering from the "idiot-savant" syndrome. These people are individuals who for the most part are severely retarded. Yet they sometimes possess astounding powers in very limited areas.

There are twins in New York who can calculate the day of the week of any date you mention. If asked in which months and years of this century the twenty-first will fall on a Thursday, the brothers can give you the correct answer instantly.

Another savant can hear a long, intricate classical piano piece for the first time and immediately sit down at a piano without the music and play it back flawlessly.

Another boy from Edinburgh, Scotland, is legally blind and so severely retarded he can barely speak. Yet he draws pictures with crayons that betray the skill of a master and are sold for exorbitant prices around the world.

The minds of savants are like calculators or tape recorders or cameras—able to capture the specific details of pictures or songs or mathematical formulas and then use those details with exacting precision.

Perhaps these examples give us a glimpse of what God originally intended our whole mind to be capable of doing.

The indications from Scripture suggest that man's capacity before the fall and his capacity once restored and glorified in heaven are unimaginable. Someone once wrote that if we were to see our glorified selves walking down the street toward us, we would be tempted to fall at our feet and worship ourselves. Such is the future of humanity in Christ.

I.   Review: Fill in the blanks.

The Doctrine of the Bible

1. R_____

2. I_____

3. I_____

4. I_____

The Doctrine of God

1. E_____

2. A_____

3. S_____

4. T_____

The Doctrine of Christ

1. D_____

2. H_____

3. R_____

4. R_____

The Doctrine of the Holy Spirit

1. P_____

2. D_____

3. S_____

4. G_____

The Doctrine of Angels

1. A_____

2. D_____

3. S_____

4. D_____

II. The Four Major Subdivisions of the Doctrine of Man Are:

1. Origin

 2. Nature

 3. Distinctiveness

 4. Destiny

(As you read the definitions of the doctrine subdivisions, notice the words in italics. Immediately following the definitions, they are repeated with blank spaces in place of the italic words. Fill in the blank spaces.)

SYMBOL:	**SUBDIVISION:**	**DEFINITION:**

1. Origin: Man was *created* by God in His image.

Origin: Man was _____ by God in His image.

Man's purpose is to "know God and enjoy Him forever." Man was *created* in perfect fellowship and harmony with God, in His image. This does not mean physical likeness, for God does not have a physical body. But it means in the psychological, emotional, and spiritual likeness of God.

CENTRAL PASSAGE:

And God created man in His own image, in the image of God He created him; male and female He created them. (Genesis 1:27)

SYMBOL:	SUBDIVISION:	DEFINITION:

2. Nature: Man has a *spiritual* as well as a physical dimension.

Nature: Man has a _____ as well as a physical dimension.

Man is *spiritual* as well as physical. Man's earthly physical body is destined to die. The moment he is born, the process is set in motion for him to die. His spirit, however, lives forever and transcends his physical limitations. After man dies, he receives a new body that lives forever.

CENTRAL PASSAGE:

Now may the God of peace Himself sanctify you entirely; and may your spirit and soul and body be preserved complete, without blame at the coming of our Lord Jesus Christ. (1 Thessalonians 5:23)

SYMBOL:	SUBDIVISION:	DEFINITION:

3. Distinctiveness: Man has *capacities* that go beyond those of any animals and mark him as the pinnacle of God's creation.

Distinctiveness: Man has _____ that go beyond those of any animals and mark him as the pinnacle of God's creation.

Man possesses intellect, emotion, and will. With intellect he can know, reason, and think.

With emotion he can feel, empathize, and experience. With will he can choose. These are all characteristics of God and, as such, are part of the "image of God" within man. They also separate man from the animals. In addition, man has the capacity for self-awareness, an awareness of God, an awareness of afterlife, and the ability to envision life in the future under different scenarios such as heaven and hell, etc. Man certainly has characteristics that overlap with the animals, but his capacities not only go beyond those of animals, he has *capacities* that no animals have.

CENTRAL PASSAGE:

Then God said, "Let Us make man in Our image, according to Our likeness; and let them rule over the fish of the sea and over the birds of the sky and over the cattle and over all the earth, and over every creeping thing that creeps on the earth." (Genesis 1:26)

SYMBOL:	**SUBDIVISION:**	**DEFINITION:**

4. Destiny: Man will live *forever* in heaven or hell.

   Destiny: Man will live _____ in heaven or hell.

Though man's spirit inhabits a body at all times, that body changes after death on earth. A new body is received, depending on his destiny, in which he will continue to live *forever.*

Destiny in hell is portrayed as agonizing torment, though little is known of the specifics of that torment. Existence in heaven is pictured in great detail, though we still might wish for more details. The heavenly body is beautiful beyond imagination, exceedingly powerful, and not subject to time and space limitations. The citizen of heaven will rule precincts of the celestial realm and will possess power, wisdom, and unbounded creativity. Greater attention will be given to man's destiny later in this chapter and in the chapter on the Doctrine of Future Things.

CENTRAL PASSAGE:

It is appointed for men to die once and after this comes judgment. (Hebrews 9:27)

The Doctrine of Man
(Write the titles of the four subdivisions on the lines below.)

SYMBOL:	**SUBDIVISION:**	**DEFINITION:**

1. O_____   Man was *created* by God in His image.

CENTRAL PASSAGE: Genesis 1:27

SYMBOL:	**SUBDIVISION:**	**DEFINITION:**

2. N_____   Man has a *spiritual* as well as a physical dimension.

CENTRAL PASSAGE: 1 Thessalonians 5:23

SYMBOL:	**SUBDIVISION:**	**DEFINITION:**

3. D_____   Man has *capacities* that go beyond those of any animals and mark him as the pinnacle of God's creation.

CENTRAL PASSAGE: Genesis 1:26

SYMBOL:	SUBDIVISION:	DEFINITION:
	4. D_____	Man will live *forever* in heaven or hell.

CENTRAL PASSAGE: Hebrews 9:27

The Doctrine of Man

(Name the four subdivisions of the Doctrine of Man and fill in the key words in the definitions.)

SYMBOL:	SUBDIVISION:	DEFINITION:
	1. _____	Man was _____ by God in His image.

CENTRAL PASSAGE: Genesis 1:27

SYMBOL:	SUBDIVISION:	DEFINITION:
	2. _____	Man has a _____ as well as a physical dimension.

CENTRAL PASSAGE: 1 Thessalonians 5:23

SYMBOL:	SUBDIVISION:	DEFINITION:
	3. _____	Man has _____ that go beyond those of any animals and mark him as the pinnacle of God's creation.

CENTRAL PASSAGE: Genesis 1:26

SYMBOL:	SUBDIVISION:	DEFINITION:

4. _____   Man will live _____ in heaven or hell.

CENTRAL PASSAGE: Hebrews 9:27

Self-Test

(Fill in the blanks.)

1. O_____   Man was _____ by God in His image.

2. N_____   Man has a _____ as well as a physical dimension.

3. D_____   Man has _____ that go beyond those of any animals and mark him as the pinnacle of God's creation.

4. D_____   Man will live _____ in heaven or hell.

Ten Great Doctrines of Systematic Theology

(From memory, fill in the names of doctrines one through six. See the Appendix for answers.)

2. _____

4. _____   3. _____

5. _____

1. _____

6. _____

THE DOCTRINE OF SIN

I grew up in rural northern Indiana where pig farming is common. I used to have to work among the pigs, feeding them, tending to their physical and medical needs, and cleaning up after them. If you have never worked around farm animals, you probably cannot imagine how bad a pen in a barn stinks when pigs have been shut up in it all winter. It will bring tears to your eyes, take your breath away, and cause you to long for a white-collar job.

But one thing I noticed. The pigs didn't mind it. I never saw a pig walk into a pen, sniff the air in disgust, and turn around and walk out because the place smelled so bad. It always seemed OK to the pig. Every pig I ever saw looked completely at home in a pigpen.

When it comes to sin, we're a little like the pigs. The smell of sin doesn't seem so bad to us. We don't even notice a lot of it. But to God, it smells like a thousand pigs that were kept in His living room for the winter.

Man does not and cannot grasp the awfulness of sin to the degree God does. But for two reasons we must try to grasp as much as we can. First, sin is harmful to us; it is self-destructive. All sins are boomerangs; they come back to hurt us every time.

Second, sin grieves God, and if we hope to live a life pleasing to Him, we must try to live a life of righteousness.

I. Review: Fill in the blanks.

The Doctrine of the Bible

1. R _____

2. I _____

3. I _____

4. I _____

The Doctrine of God

1. E _____

2. A _____

3. S _____

4. T _____

The Doctrine of Christ

1. D _____

2. H _____

3. R _____

4. R _____

The Doctrine of the Holy Spirit

1. P _____

2. D _____

3. S _____

4. G _____

The Doctrine of Angels

1. A _____

2. D _____

3. S _____

4. D _____

The Doctrine of Man

1. O _____

2. N _____

3. D _____

4. D _____

II. The Four Major Subdivisions of the Doctrine of Sin Are:

 1. Nature

 2. Fall

 3. Corruption

4. Rebellion

(As you read the definitions of the doctrine subdivisions, notice the words in italics. Immediately following the definitions, they are repeated with blank spaces in place of the italic words. Fill in the blank spaces.)

SYMBOL: **SUBDIVISION:**   **DEFINITION:**

1. Nature: Sin is any lack of conformity to the moral *perfection* of God.

Nature: Sin is any lack of conformity to the moral _____ of God.

All that is good, right, and pleasant comes from God. Anything that does not come from God is the opposite. By definition, it must be bad, wrong, and unpleasant. We are creatures who sin. When we do, we bring bad, wrong, and unpleasant things into our lives, we diminish the reputation of God as His children, and we decrease the interest the non-Christian world might have in God because they do not see the difference between being Christian and not being Christian.

CENTRAL PASSAGE:

All unrighteousness is sin. (1 John 5:17)

SYMBOL: **SUBDIVISION:**   **DEFINITION:**

2. Fall: The *separation* of Adam and Eve from God in the Garden of Eden because of original sin.

Fall: The _____ of Adam and
                Eve from God in the Garden of
                Eden because of original sin.

All the pain, all the evil, all the suffering that
is in the world, that has ever been in the world,
and that will ever be in the world can be traced
back to one event: when Adam and Eve disobeyed God in the Garden. Because of the
cataclysmically negative effects of that event,
it has been referred to as the fall of man.

CENTRAL PASSAGE:

When the woman saw that the tree was good for
food, and that it was a delight to the eyes, and that
the tree was desirable to make one wise, she took
from its fruit and ate; and she gave also to her
husband with her, and he ate. (Genesis 3:6)

SYMBOL: **SUBDIVISION:**   **DEFINITION:**

3. Corruption: Mankind as a whole was *corrupted*
                 by the original fall.

   Corruption: Mankind as a whole was _____
                 by the original fall.

Sin entered mankind, and now all men are corrupted with sin. It is not that man is not capable
of doing good (for certainly some people do
wonderful things), or even that he is as bad as
he could be (many people could be much worse
than they are). It is just that he cannot keep
from doing that which is bad, because his essential nature has been corrupted. David said,
"in sin my mother conceived me" (Psalm 51:5).
This does not mean that his mother sinned, but
that all men are born sinners. We are not sinners because we sin. We sin because we are
sinners.

CENTRAL PASSAGE:

And you were dead in your trespasses and sins. . . . Among them we too all formerly lived in the lusts of our flesh, indulging in the desires of the flesh and of the mind, and were by nature children of wrath. (Ephesians 2:1, 3)

SYMBOL:	**SUBDIVISION:**	**DEFINITION:**

4. Rebellion: Because man's internal nature has been corrupted by sin, he cannot keep from committing *personal* sins.

Rebellion: Because man's internal nature has been corrupted by sin, he cannot keep from committing _____ sins.

Man's heart has been corrupted and therefore, he commits individual, personal sins. Some of these sins are sins of commission (things we ought not to do, but do) and some are sins of omission (things we ought to do but don't). They may be tangible acts, or they may be deficient attitudes, motives, or perspectives. When we compare ourselves with other people on external things, we might not do so badly. But when we compare ourselves with Jesus, who had no imperfections in act, thought, motive, word, or deed, we see that we fall short.

CENTRAL PASSAGES:

For all have sinned and fall short of the glory of God. . . . For the wages of sin is death. (Romans 3:23 and 6:23)

The Doctrine of Sin

(Write the titles of the four subdivisions on the lines below.)

SYMBOL:	SUBDIVISION:	DEFINITION:

1. N_____   Sin is any lack of conformity to the moral *perfection* of God.

CENTRAL PASSAGE: 1 John 5:17

SYMBOL:	SUBDIVISION:	DEFINITION:

2. F_____   The *separation* of Adam and Eve from God in the Garden of Eden because of original sin.

CENTRAL PASSAGE: Genesis 3:6

SYMBOL:	SUBDIVISION:	DEFINITION:

3. C_____   Mankind as a whole was *corrupted* by the original fall.

CENTRAL PASSAGE: Ephesians 2:1, 3

SYMBOL:	SUBDIVISION:	DEFINITION:

4. R_____   Because man's internal nature has been corrupted by sin, he cannot keep from committing *personal* sins.

CENTRAL PASSAGES: Romans 3:23 and 6:23

The Doctrine of Sin

(Name the four subdivisions of the Doctrine of Sin and fill in the key words in the definitions.)

SYMBOL: **SUBDIVISION:** **DEFINITION:**

1. _____ Sin is any lack of conformity to the moral _____ of God.

CENTRAL PASSAGE: 1 John 5:17

SYMBOL: **SUBDIVISION:** **DEFINITION:**

2. _____ The _____ of Adam and Eve from God in the Garden of Eden because of original sin.

CENTRAL PASSAGE: Genesis 3:6

SYMBOL: **SUBDIVISION:** **DEFINITION:**

3. _____ Mankind as a whole was _____ by the original fall.

CENTRAL PASSAGE: Ephesians 2:1, 3

SYMBOL: **SUBDIVISION:** **DEFINITION:**

4. _____ Because man's internal nature has been corrupted by sin, he cannot keep from committing _____ sins.

CENTRAL PASSAGES: Romans 3:23 and 6:23

Self-Test

(Fill in the blanks.)

1. N_____ Sin is any lack of conformity to the moral _____ of God.

2. F_____ The _____ of Adam and Eve from God in the Garden of Eden because of original sin.

3. C_____   Mankind as a whole was _____ by the original fall.

4. R_____   Because man's internal nature has been corrupted by sin, he cannot keep from committing _____ sins.

Ten Great Doctrines of Systematic Theology

(From memory, fill in the names of doctrines one through seven. See the Appendix for answers.)

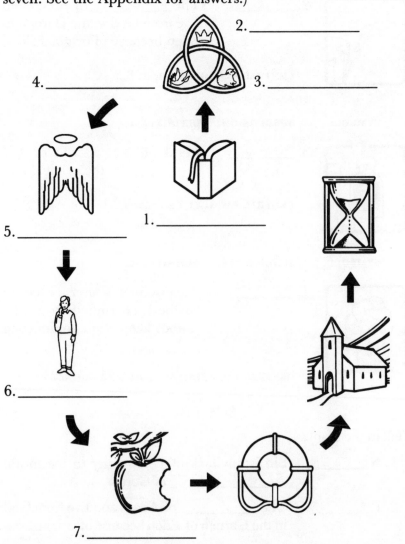

2. _____

4. _____   3. _____

5. _____   1. _____

6. _____

7. _____

THE DOCTRINE OF SALVATION

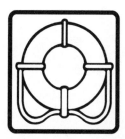

In studying the matter of man's destiny, we actually overlap with our overview of the Doctrine of Salvation. We saw earlier that man has a spirit as well as a body and that he will live forever in heaven or hell. The immediate concern, then, is what determines his destiny? The Bible appears to teach that children who die before the age of accountability, that is, the age at which they have the intellectual capacity to accept or reject God, go to heaven. After they reach that age, if they do not accept God's salvation before they die, they will go to hell. How, then, does man avoid that destiny? What is the basis of God's salvation?

There are several commonly held beliefs about how to get to heaven. One belief suggests that if no really terrible sins are committed, God will overlook the small ones. Another suggests that if your good works outweigh your bad works at the end of your life, you will make it to heaven. Still another suggests that God will line up all the people in the world who ever lived, from the worst to the best, and divide that line in half. The worst go to hell, and the best go to heaven. All these beliefs are incorrect. Good and bad works have absolutely nothing to do with whether or not you go to heaven.

I.   Review: Fill in the blanks.

The Doctrine of the Bible

1. R_____

2. I_____

3. I_____

4. I_____

The Doctrine of God

1. E_____

2. A_____

3. S_____

4. T_____

The Doctrine of Christ

1. D_____

2. H_____

3. R_____

4. R_____

The Doctrine of the Holy Spirit

1. P_____

2. D_____

3. S_____

4. G_____

The Doctrine of Angels

1. A_____

2. D_____

3. S_____

4. D_____

The Doctrine of Man

1. O_____

2. N_____

3. D_____

4. D_____

The Doctrine of Sin

1. N_____

2. F_____

3. C_____

4. R_____

II. **The Four Major Subdivisions of the Doctrine of Salvation Are:**

1. Basis

2. Result

3. Cost

4. Timing

(As you read the definitions of the doctrine subdivisions, notice the words in italics. Immediately following the definitions, they are repeated with blank spaces in place of the italic words. Fill in the blank spaces.)

SYMBOL:	SUBDIVISION:	DEFINITION:
	1. Basis:	Salvation is a *gift* God gives to those who believe.
	Basis:	Salvation is a _____ God gives to those who believe.

We cannot earn our salvation. We are imperfect, and we cannot make ourselves perfect. Yet God demands perfection. Therefore, all we can do is cast ourselves on God's mercy. In His mercy, God offers to forgive our sin and *give* us a new nature of holiness so that we can be in perfect relationship with Him. The completion of that relationship is not realized until we die and we shed the "body of sin" in which we live. God's offer has one condition: that we believe in and receive Jesus as our Savior.

CENTRAL PASSAGE:

For by grace you have been saved through faith; and that not of yourselves, it is the gift of God; not as a result of works, that no one should boast. (Ephesians 2:8–9)

| SYMBOL: | SUBDIVISION: | DEFINITION: |

2. Result:

God extends *forgiveness* of sin and eternal life to those who accept Him.

Result:

God extends _____ of sin and eternal life to those who accept Him.

God's solution to man's inherent dilemma is to offer him *forgiveness* of his sins and to give him a new nature that is not flawed. Man still languishes under the impact of sin until his flawed body dies and he receives a new body. Then he is free to serve God forever in heaven in undiluted righteousness.

CENTRAL PASSAGE:

Therefore having been justified by faith, we have peace with God through our Lord Jesus Christ. (Romans 5:1)

| SYMBOL: | SUBDIVISION: | DEFINITION: |

3. Cost:

The penalty of sin is paid for by the *substitutionary* death of Christ.

Cost:

The penalty of sin is paid for by the _____ death of Christ.

Sin brings death. Since all have sinned, all have died, spiritually, and are separated from God. Jesus was without sin, and He willingly died with the understanding that His death could count as a *substitution* for our own. If you believe in Jesus and receive Him as your personal Savior, God will then count His death for yours and give you eternal life.

CENTRAL PASSAGE:

For Christ also died for sins once for all, the just for the unjust, in order that He might bring us to God, having been put to death in the flesh, but made alive in the spirit. (1 Peter 3:18)

SYMBOL: **SUBDIVISION:**   **DEFINITION:**

4. Timing: Our salvation is completed at the *death* of the *body*.

Timing: Our salvation is completed at the _____ of the_____.

Man is body and spirit. Upon becoming a Christian, a person's spirit is born again and he is given eternal life. His body, at that point, remains unchanged. It is corrupted by sin, is susceptible to disease and death, and is inclined to sin. The brain, which is part of the physical body, is still encumbered with old programming that is counter to biblical truth. Because of this, the Christian experiences a continuous struggle between the new inner man who wishes to serve God and the outer man who feels the pull to sin (see Romans 7). This conflict continues until the *death* of the *body*, at which time the spirit of the Christian is transported immediately to heaven to receive a new body, untouched by sin. (Rom. 8:23)

Fortunately, until our salvation is completed with "the redemption of the body," when we sin after having become a Christian "we have an advocate with the Father, Jesus Christ the righteous" (1 John 2:1). "If we confess our sins, He is faithful and righteous to forgive us our sins and to cleanse us from all unrighteousness" (1 John 1:9). God does not want us to sin, but He recognizes that as long as we are in this body, we will. When we do, He cleanses us. The death of Christ on the cross was sufficient for all our sins, past and future. God is continuously working in our lives, however, to lead us to a more righteous lifestyle. If we resist this work of God, He chastens us, as any loving father would a child, to correct inappropriate behavior. (See Heb. 12:4–13.)

CENTRAL PASSAGE:

And not only this, but also we ourselves, having the first fruits of the Spirit, even we ourselves groan within ourselves, waiting eagerly for our adoption as sons, the redemption of our body. (Romans 8:23)

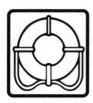

The Doctrine of Salvation

(Write the titles of the four subdivisions on the lines below.)

SYMBOL:	**SUBDIVISION:**	**DEFINITION:**

1. B_____ Salvation is a *gift* God gives to those who believe.

CENTRAL PASSAGE: Ephesians 2:8–9

SYMBOL:	**SUBDIVISION:**	**DEFINITION:**

2. R_____ God extends *forgiveness* of sin and eternal life to those who accept Him.

CENTRAL PASSAGE: Romans 5:1

SYMBOL: **SUBDIVISION:**   **DEFINITION:**

3. C_____   The penalty of sin is paid for by the *substitutionary* death of Christ.

CENTRAL PASSAGE: 1 Peter 3:18

SYMBOL: **SUBDIVISION:**   **DEFINITION:**

4. T_____   Our salvation is completed at the *death* of the *body*.

CENTRAL PASSAGE: Romans 8:23

The Doctrine of Salvation

(Name the four subdivisions of the Doctrine of Salvation and fill in the key words in the definition.)

SYMBOL: **SUBDIVISION:**   **DEFINITION:**

1. _____   Salvation is a _____ God gives to those who believe.

CENTRAL PASSAGE: Ephesians 2:8–9

SYMBOL: **SUBDIVISION:**   **DEFINITION:**

2. _____   God extends _____ of sin and eternal life to those who accept Him.

CENTRAL PASSAGE: Romans 5:1

SYMBOL:	SUBDIVISION:	DEFINITION:

3. _____   The penalty of sin is paid for by the _____ death of Christ.

CENTRAL PASSAGE: 1 Peter 3:18

SYMBOL:	SUBDIVISION:	DEFINITION:

4. _____   Our salvation is completed at the _____ of the _____.

CENTRAL PASSAGE: Romans 8:23

Self-Test

(Fill in the blanks.)

1. B_____   Salvation is a _____ God gives to those who believe.

2. R_____   God extends _____ of sin and eternal life to those who accept Him.

3. C_____   The penalty of sin is paid for by the _____ death of Christ.

4. T_____   Our salvation is completed at the _____ of the _____ .

Ten Great Doctrines of Systematic Theology

(From memory, fill in the names of doctrines one through eight. See the Appendix for answers.)

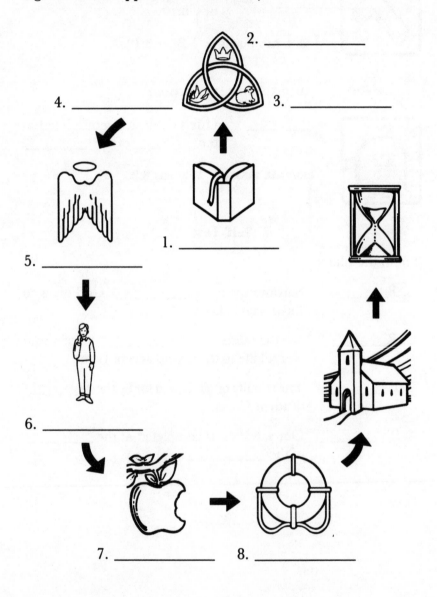

2. _____

4. _____   3. _____

5. _____

1. _____

6. _____

7. _____   8. _____

NINE

THE DOCTRINE OF
THE CHURCH

The Church is to be the physical representation of Christ on earth now that He has returned to heaven. What Christ said, we are to say. What Christ did, we are to do. The message Christ proclaimed, we are to proclaim, and the character Christ manifested, we are to manifest. The world can no longer see Christ living on earth. He is removed, physically, though He lives in the hearts of His children. Because the world can no longer see Christ living on earth, it should be able to get a pretty good idea of Christ by looking at His Church.

The Church is a wonderfully important institution that has fallen into some disregard in the United States lately, even among Christians. It happened partially because many in the mainline denominations abandoned the historic fundamentals of the faith for a form of Christianity that denied the very things that were distinctive to Christianity. When that happened, the church lost its justification for its existence, and attendance began to drop precipitously.

Then a remnant church exerted itself; it was made up of largely newer denominations and independent churches as well as some churches and denominations that had held firm or renewed themselves. The renewed churches disdained the theological shallowness of churches that had denied their faith and, as a result, they "threw the baby out with the bath water." Out with the theological shallowness went deep respect for tradition, church authority, and the clergy.

But, as Augustine said, "He cannot have God for his father who does not have the church for his mother." The time has come for a resurgence of respect for the Church, the Great Bride of Christ, and to hold her with the same regard with which God holds her. The time has come to believe Jesus' promise: "I will build My church." We humbly ask Him, "What would you have me to do?"

I. Review: Fill in the blanks.

The Doctrine of the Bible

1. R_____

2. I_____

3. I_____

4. I_____

The Doctrine of God

1. E_____

2. A_____

3. S_____

4. T_____

The Doctrine of Christ

1. D_____

2. H_____

3. R_____

4. R_____

The Doctrine of the Holy Spirit

1. P_____

2. D_____

3. S_____

4. G_____

The Doctrine of Angels

1. A_____

2. D_____

3. S_____

4. D_____

The Doctrine of Man

1. O_____

2. N_____

3. D_____

4. D_____

The Doctrine of Sin

1. N_____

2. F_____

3. C_____

4. R_____

The Doctrine of Salvation

1. B_____

2. R_____

3. C_____

4. T_____

II. The Four Major Subdivisions of the Doctrine of the Church Are:

1. Universal Church

2. Local Church

3. Leadership

4. Membership

(As you read the definitions of the doctrine subdivisions, notice the words in italics. Immediately following the definitions, they are repeated with blank spaces in place of the italic words. Fill in the blank spaces.)

SYMBOL:	SUBDIVISION:	DEFINITION:
	1. Universal Church:	The Universal Church is the totality of all *believers* in Jesus.
	Universal Church:	The Universal Church is the totality of all _____ in Jesus.

The Universal Church, also called the Body of Christ (Col. 1:24), refers to all people in all parts of the world who have become Christians since the beginning of the Church and who will become Christians before Christ returns. The Church began on the day of Pentecost (Acts 2), and will culminate when Christ returns. Christ is the head of the church (Col. 1:18), and the Universal Church is to be the representation of Christ on earth, collectively doing His will.

CENTRAL PASSAGE:

Husbands, love your wives, just as Christ also loved the church and gave Himself up for her; . . . that He might present to Himself the church in all her glory, having no spot or wrinkle or any such thing; but that she should be holy and blameless. (Ephesians 5:25, 27)

SYMBOL: **SUBDIVISION:**   **DEFINITION:**

2. Local Church: A local assembly of believers *organized* to carry out the responsibilities of the Universal Church.

Local Church: A local assembly of believers _____ to carry out the responsibilities of the Universal Church.

The church is not a building, but people. At any given time and place, Christians are to band together to carry out the responsibilities of the Universal Church. As such, they organize to govern themselves, select spiritual leaders, collect money for ministry, observe baptism and communion, exercise church discipline, engage in mutual edification and evangelism, and worship of God.

CENTRAL PASSAGE:

Paul, called as an apostle of Jesus Christ by the will of God, . . . to the church of God which is at Corinth. (1 Corinthians 1–2)

SYMBOL:	SUBDIVISION:	DEFINITION:

3. Leadership: Those in the church worthy of being followed because of their *spiritual* maturity.

Leadership: Those in the church worthy of being followed because of their _____ maturity.

Leadership in the local church is invested in pastor-teachers, elders, and deacons and deaconesses. The Scripture appears to give freedom as to how this leadership is organized and functions, but it is quite specific about the spiritual qualifications. Only spiritually mature people are to be given high positions of spiritual leadership in the church.

CENTRAL PASSAGE:

An overseer, then, must be above reproach, the husband of one wife, temperate, prudent, respectable, hospitable, able to teach, not addicted to wine or pugnacious, but gentle, uncontentious, free from the love of money. He must be one who manages his own household well, keeping his children under control with all dignity . . . and not a new convert, . . . and he must have a good reputation with those outside the church. (1 Timothy 3:2–4, 6–7)

SYMBOL:	SUBDIVISION:	DEFINITION:

4. Membership: *Belonging* to the Universal Church and a local church.

Membership: _____ to the Universal Church and a local church.

When a person becomes a Christian, he or she immediately and automatically becomes a member of the Universal Church, the Body of Christ. Throughout church history, local churches have had varying requirements for membership that range from very limited to very strict. This appears to be a point of freedom given local churches in the Scripture. An important point, however, is that everyone should be a part of a local church. God never intended for Christians to try to make it alone. Placing oneself under spiritual authority and in mutual ministry with others is essential to spiritual health.

CENTRAL PASSAGE:

Let us consider how to stimulate one another to love and good deeds, not forsaking our own assembling together, as is the habit of some, but encouraging one another; and all the more, as you see the day drawing near. (Hebrews 10:24–25)

The Doctrine of the Church

(Write the titles of the four subdivisions on the lines below.)

SYMBOL: **SUBDIVISION:**   **DEFINITION:**

1. U_____   The Universal Church is the totality of all *believers* in Jesus.

CENTRAL PASSAGE: Ephesians 5:25, 27

SYMBOL: **SUBDIVISION:**   **DEFINITION:**

2. L _____   A local assembly of believers *organized* to carry out the responsibilities of the Universal Church.

CENTRAL PASSAGE: 1 Corinthians 1–2

| SYMBOL: | SUBDIVISION: | DEFINITION: |

3. L _____   Those in the church worthy of being followed because of their *spiritual* maturity.

CENTRAL PASSAGE: 1 Timothy 3:2–4, 6–7

| SYMBOL: | SUBDIVISION: | DEFINITION: |

4. M _____   *Belonging* to the Universal Church and a local church.

CENTRAL PASSAGE: Hebrews 10:24–25

The Doctrine of the Church

(Name the four subdivisions of the Doctrine of Church and fill in the key words in the definitions.)

| SYMBOL: | SUBDIVISION: | DEFINITION: |

1. _____   The Universal Church is the totality of all _____ in Jesus.

CENTRAL PASSAGE: Ephesians 5:25, 27

| SYMBOL: | SUBDIVISION: | DEFINITION: |

2. _____   A local assembly of believers _____ to carry out the responsibilities of the Universal Church.

CENTRAL PASSAGE: 1 Corinthians 1–2

SYMBOL:	SUBDIVISION:	DEFINITION:

3. _____ Those in the church worthy of being followed because of their _____ maturity.

CENTRAL PASSAGE: 1 Timothy 3:2–4, 6–7

SYMBOL:	SUBDIVISION:	DEFINITION:

4. _____ _____ to the Universal Church and a local church.

CENTRAL PASSAGE: Hebrews 10:24–25

Self-Test

(Fill in the blanks.)

1. B_____ The Universal Church is the totality of all _____ in Jesus.

2. O_____ A local assembly of believers _____ to carry out the responsibilities of the Universal Church.

3. S_____ Those in the church worthy of being followed because of their _____ maturity.

4. B_____ _____ to the Universal Church and a local church.

Ten Great Doctrines of Systematic Theology

(From memory, fill in the names of doctrines one through nine. See the Appendix for answers.)

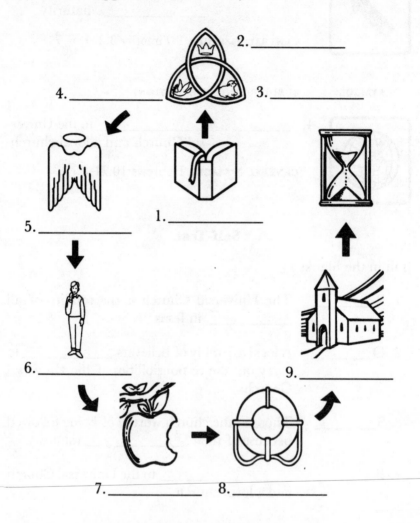

THE DOCTRINE OF FUTURE THINGS

The story of Little Lord Fauntleroy is an engaging and instructive one. The son of an English earl marries an American woman and is consequently disinherited. Some years later, he dies at sea and his widow and son live humbly in New York City. The disinherited man's father, the Earl of Darringcourt, becomes aged and is concerned for the succession to his fortune and family line. His ten-year-old American grandson is his only legal heir, so he sends a representative to America to offer to have his grandson come to live on the fabulous estate as Lord Fauntleroy and eventually succeed him as Earl of Darringcourt. There is one catch. Little Lord Fauntleroy's American mother, who was the cause of the original disinheritance, an exemplary woman with whom Lord Fauntleroy is very close, cannot live on the estate. The story of the initial conflict and misunderstanding, and the subsequent healing and restoration of relationships is a touching one in which everyone eventually lives happily ever after.

When the Earl of Darringcourt's representative first comes to America with the proposal, a circumstance arises that is analogous to the life of a Christian. He describes what life will be like as Lord Fauntleroy. Wealth, power, honor, glory are his. He is a royal heir. Yet he will have to wait until he gets to England to experience it. For now, he will have some limited benefits, but for the most part, until he crosses the Atlantic, the life of Lord Fauntleroy has to wait.

The situation for the Christian is similar. The Bible presents a picture of a future that is difficult to imagine. Power, glory, wealth, and honor are ours. But in large measure, we must wait until we get to heaven to experience it. For now, the limitations of earth are very much with us. Until we cross the Atlantic, the life of Lord Fauntleroy will have to wait.

The information the Bible presents about Future Things is sketchy. The prophetic information in the Bible is not given to satisfy our innate curiosity about the future, but to encourage us to live like royalty while we are still here on earth. It is given, not to impact our curiosity, but our lifestyle.

Therefore, while the information is incomplete as to details we might desire to know, it is adequate for us to take our present life seriously. We are royalty with a celestial inheritance, but we are presently misplaced.

I. **Review:** Fill in the blanks.

The Doctrine of the Bible

1. R_____

2. I_____

3. I_____

4. I_____

The Doctrine of God

1. E_____

2. A_____

3. S_____

4. T_____

The Doctrine of Christ

1. D_____

2. H_____

3. R_____

4. R_____

The Doctrine of the Holy Spirit

1. P_____

2. D_____

3. S_____

4. G_____

The Doctrine of Angels

1. A_____

2. D_____

3. S_____

4. D_____

The Doctrine of Man

1. O_____

2. N_____

3. D_____

4. D_____

The Doctrine of Sin

1. N_____

2. F_____

3. C_____

4. R_____

The Doctrine of Salvation

1. B_____

2. R_____

3. C_____

4. T_____

The Doctrine of the Church

1. U_____

2. L_____

3. L_____

4. M_____

II. The Four Major Subdivisions of the Doctrine of Future Things Are:

1. Return

2. Judgment

3. Universe

 4. Eternity

(As you read the definitions of the doctrine subdivisions, notice the words in italics. Immediately following the definitions, they are repeated with blank spaces in place of the italic words. Fill in the blank spaces.)

SYMBOL:	SUBDIVISION:	DEFINITION:

1. Return: Jesus will *return* to earth again.

   Return: Jesus will _____ to earth again.

Jesus of Nazareth was crucified, buried, and resurrected about A.D. 30. He ascended into heaven where He has remained for the last two thousand years. At some time in the future, and from prophetic information it could be at any time, He will *return* to earth. When He does, it will not be as a carpenter's son but in power and glory, revealing His true cosmic sovereignty. During His first visit to earth, He came as a servant with an emphasis on His humanity. During His second visit to earth He will come as a king, emphasizing His deity.

CENTRAL PASSAGE:

For the Son of Man is going to come in the glory of His Father with His angels. (Matthew 16:27)

SYMBOL:	SUBDIVISION:	DEFINITION:

2. Judgment: God will *confirm* the eternal *destiny* of all individuals.

Judgment: God will _____ the eternal _____ of all individuals.

At two different times and places, God will conduct audiences with all humanity to *confirm* our eternal *destiny*. Those who believed in Jesus and received Him will then be confirmed to eternity in heaven with Him. Those who did not believe in Him and receive Him will be confirmed to eternal separation from Him in hell.

CENTRAL PASSAGES:

For we must all appear before the judgment seat of Christ, that each one may be recompensed for his deeds in the body, according to what he has done, whether good or bad. (2 Corinthians 5:10)

And if anyone's name was not found written in the book of life, he was thrown into the lake of fire. (Revelation 20:15)

SYMBOL:	SUBDIVISION:	DEFINITION:

3. Universe: The old universe will be destroyed and *replaced* with a new one.

Universe: The old universe will be destroyed and _____ with a new one.

The present universe was flawed with sin at the time of the "fall" of man. While much of nature is beautiful, much of it is also destructive and uninhabitable. The universe will be destroyed with an apocalyptic cosmic fire and *replaced* with a new universe and a new earth that will have no harmful features. (See 2 Pet. 3:12–13 and Rev. 21:4.)

CENTRAL PASSAGE:

And I saw a new heaven and a new earth; for the first heaven and the first earth passed away, and there is no longer any sea. (Revelation 21:1)

SYMBOL:	**SUBDIVISION:**	**DEFINITION:**

4. Eternity: Christians will live with God *forever.*

Eternity: Christians will live with God _____.

Jesus will reign in absolute righteousness. Only goodness and beauty will exist. Believers will rule with Him *forever* as vice-regents. They will govern angelic beings. They will be beings of beauty and power who will participate in glorious celestial ceremonies. Believers themselves will receive much personal glory by the grace and goodness of God, as well as spend generous time worshiping and praising God. Intellect, beauty, power, and talent will be virtually limitless as believers both serve Jesus the King and rule with Him in a world that progressively glorifies God and brings great joy and individual satisfaction.

CENTRAL PASSAGES:

In My Father's house are many dwelling places; if it were not so, I would have told you; for I go to prepare a place for you. And if I go and prepare a place for you, I will come again, and receive you to Myself; that where I am, there you may be also. (John 14:2–3)

And they [Christians] shall reign forever and ever. (Revelation 22:5)

The Doctrine of Future Things

(Write the titles of the four subdivisions on the lines below.)

SYMBOL: **SUBDIVISION:**   **DEFINITION:**

1. R_____   Jesus will *return* to earth again.

CENTRAL PASSAGE: Matthew 16:27

SYMBOL: **SUBDIVISION:**   **DEFINITION:**

2. J_____   God will *confirm* the eternal *destiny* of all individuals.

CENTRAL PASSAGES: 2 Corinthians 5:10
                     Revelation 20:15

SYMBOL: **SUBDIVISION:**   **DEFINITION:**

3. U_____   The old universe will be destroyed and *replaced* with a new one.

CENTRAL PASSAGE: Revelation 21:1

SYMBOL: **SUBDIVISION:**   **DEFINITION:**

4. E_____   Christians will live with God *forever.*

CENTRAL PASSAGES: John 14:2–3
                     Revelation 22:5

The Doctrine of Future Things

(Name the four subdivisions of the Doctrine of Future Things and fill in the key words in the definitions.)

SYMBOL: **SUBDIVISION:**   **DEFINITION:**

1. _____   Jesus will _____ to earth again.

CENTRAL PASSAGE: Matthew 16:27

SYMBOL: **SUBDIVISION:**   **DEFINITION:**

2. _____   God will _____ the eternal _____ of all individuals.

CENTRAL PASSAGES: 2 Corinthians 5:10
Revelation 20:15

SYMBOL: **SUBDIVISION:**   **DEFINITION:**

3. _____   The old universe will be destroyed and _____ with a new one.

CENTRAL PASSAGE: Revelation 21:1

SYMBOL: **SUBDIVISION:**   **DEFINITION:**

4. _____   Christians will live with God _____.

CENTRAL PASSAGES: John 14:2–3
Revelation 22:5

Self-Test

(Fill in the blanks.)

1. R_____   Jesus will _____ to earth again.

2. J_____ God will _____ the eternal _____ of all individuals.

3. U_____ The old universe will be destroyed and _____ with a new one.

4. E_____ Christians will live with God _____.

Ten Great Doctrines of Systematic Theology

(From memory, fill in the names of all the doctrines. See the Appendix for answers.)

2. _____

4. _____   3. _____

1. _____

5. _____   10. _____

6. _____   9. _____

Fill in the names of the doctrines and their subdivisions on the lines below:

1. B _____

    R_____

    I _____

    I _____

    I _____

2. G _____

    E _____

    A_____

    S _____

    T_____

3. C _____

    D_____

    H_____

    R_____

    R_____

4. H_____   S_____

    P _____

    D_____

    S _____

    G_____

5. A _____

    A _____

    D _____

    S _____

    D _____

6. M _____

    O _____

    N _____

    D _____

    D _____

7. S _____

    N _____

    F _____

    C _____

    R _____

8. S _____

    B _____

    R _____

    C _____

    T _____

9. C _____

    U _____

    L _____

    L _____

    M _____

10. F_____ T_____

    R _____

    J _____

    U _____

    E _____

Congratulations! You have just completed an overview of the ten major doctrines of systematic theology. There is still much more about Bible doctrines to be learned. In a sense, you have learned a very broad outline, and much of the Bible is dedicated to filling in the outline. Nevertheless, you now have a structure for acquiring an advanced knowledge of the doctrines of the Bible. We will now look at ten great subjects of biblical theology.

TEN GREAT SUBJECTS OF BIBLICAL THEOLOGY

UNITY

CENTRAL PASSAGE: Behold, how good and how pleasant it is / For brothers to dwell together in unity!

Psalm 133:1

In the dark days of World War II, Hitler had the British army on French soil, backed up against the English Channel, and was pressing down on them for the kill. Thousands of English soldiers would die if they could not be evacuated; yet evacuation seemed impossible. There were not enough ships to evacuate them before the German army reached them.

Somehow the word of the predicament spread throughout England, and everyone with a boat responded—from large military craft to ferries to personal sailboats to personally owned fishing boats, all of England! They crossed the English Channel, loaded as many soldiers as they could hold, took them back across the Channel to England, and then returned for another load. Through this remarkable experience of national unity, the British army was saved. The nation throbbed with exultation. By acting as one, the impossible was accomplished and joy reigned unchecked.

Unity is one of the great experiences of life. We have all seen the unity of an Olympic team or the joy of unity in the marriage ceremony or the unity of soldiers fighting a common enemy. It is inherently a joyous thing to experience unity with others . . . perhaps the greatest joy in life.

Unity is one of the great themes of the Bible. In the Old Testament, we read, "Hear, O Israel! The LORD is our God, the

Lord is one!" (Deut. 6:4). "Behold, how good and how pleasant it is / For brothers to dwell together in unity!" David declares in Psalm 133:1. God wanted the entire nation of Israel to be united in following the Law and to be "one" in following Him.

In the New Testament, the theme is developed even more fully. Jesus prays, in His prayer in John 17:22, that "they [His followers] may be one." In Ephesians 4:3 we read, "[be] diligent to preserve the unity of the Spirit in the bond of peace." The apostle Paul then goes on to explain that spiritual gifts are given to the Church for the building up of the body of Christ, "until we all attain to the unity of the faith" (Eph. 4:13).

In a similar vein, Paul instructs the Christians in Colossi to exercise love toward one another, "which is the perfect bond of unity" (Col. 3:14). When you consider the inter-relatedness of love, peace, and harmony with unity, you see that unity is a dominant theme running throughout the Bible. God is *One*, and He wants His people to be *one*.

Also throughout the Bible we see that God is a picturing God. God gives us physical pictures on earth to help us see and understand spiritual things in heaven. That is one reason He wants His children to live in unity. The Bible pictures accurately the unity that exists in the godhead. By living in unity, His children experience what it is to be like God.

Also, when Christians live in unity, it shows the world what God is like. The love, mutual respect, deference, and fellowship shared by God's children as they live together in unity show the world that God is a God of love, respect, and fellowship, and it creates in the hearts of the people observing this unity a desire to know the God who created it.

In summary, unity is a dominant theme in the Bible because when God's people live together in unity they experience the greatest personal joy as they accurately reflect to the world what God is like. These united Christians create a hunger and thirst in the minds of unbelievers to know God because of what they see of Him in His children. Unity is no small thing.

1. What makes true unity possible?

True unity already *exists* because we are one in Christ.

CENTRAL PASSAGE: [Be] diligent to preserve the unity of the Spirit in the bond of peace. (Ephesians 4:3)

True unity already exists. It is not something we have to manufacture or something that disappears if we somehow fail. God's children are spiritually united in Christ just as surely as the six children of my mother and father (of whom I am number six) are united, even though, while we were growing up, we sometimes acted in an ununited way. In fact, there were times when homicide seemed just around the corner! But that did not change the fact that we were united, as brothers and sister, in the blood of our parents.

Now that we are all adults, functional unity abounds. When we get together for family visits, which occur infrequently because several siblings live in other parts of the country, there is none of the squabbling and infighting that sometimes characterized our childhood relationships. Now it is all fellowship and fun; we manifest in our relationships the true unity that exists in our common lineage.

The same is true of the Church of Christ; we have true unity because of our common lineage in Christ. Our great challenge in life is to manifest this true unity on a functional, practical level.

The apostle Paul writes in Ephesians,

> You are fellow citizens with the saints, and are of God's household, having been built upon the foundation of the apostles and prophets, Christ Jesus Himself being the corner stone, in whom the whole building, being fitted together is growing into a holy temple in the Lord; in whom you also are being built together into a dwelling of God in the Spirit. (2:19–22)

In this passage our unity is likened to the unity that exists among all the stones in a building: each separate and yet united in that they are all part of a larger whole.

Paul reinforces this when he says in Ephesians 4:3, "[be] diligent to preserve the unity of the Spirit in the bond of peace." Notice that he does not say *create* the unity. He says *preserve* the unity. It already exists. Our task is to manifest in our lifestyles the inner spiritual unity that already exists.

Q. What makes unity possible?
A. True unity already _____ because we are one in Christ.

2. How is functional unity established?

It is established by common *beliefs*.

CENTRAL PASSAGE: There is one body and one Spirit, just as also you were called in one hope of your calling; one Lord, one faith, one baptism, one God and Father of all who is over all and through all and in all. (Ephesians 4:4–6)

Functional unity is established first by common belief. Since this is true, the ones who are united are those who have embraced these beliefs. They must believe in the one God and in the one Lord, Jesus. They must hold to the one faith that, as Jude 3 says, "was once for all delivered to the saints." When we believe in Christ, we become adopted into His family, becoming spiritual brothers and sisters with one another, members of the Body of Christ. This establishes a spiritual unity with all who believe, and this unity exists, as I said earlier, regardless of whether the brothers and sisters act in a unified way.

Q. How is functional unity established?
A. It is established by common _____.

3. How is functional unity maintained?

It is maintained by mutual *submission* in love.

CENTRAL PASSAGE: Do nothing from selfishness or empty conceit, but with humility of mind let each of you regard one another as more important than himself; do not merely look out for your own personal interests, but also for the interests of others. (Philippians 2:3–4)

Maintaining the unity is easier said than done. You have probably heard the bad joke, "To live above with saints we love, oh, that will be glory. To live below with saints we know, well, that's another story!"

Just because we are spiritually related with one another and spiritually united in Christ does not mean it is always easy to act in a united way. So how do we maintain unity with so many forces working against us?

The answer is *selflessness*. It's sort of like saying $E=MC^2$. It is simple, yet few people understand it. Selflessness is simple, too, yet few people find selflessness easy to live out.

There are many ways of saying selflessness. *Love,* for example, is another way of saying selflessness. The apostle Paul wrote in Philippians 2:2–4:

Make my joy complete by being of the same mind, maintaining the same love, united in spirit, intent on one purpose. Do nothing from selfishness or empty conceit, but with humility of mind let each of you regard one another as more important than himself; do not merely look out for your own personal interests, but also for the interests of others.

This is selflessness. The apostle Paul said, "Love does no wrong to a neighbor; love therefore is the fulfillment of the law" (Rom. 13:10). Doing no harm to your neighbor is selflessness.

Servanthood is another way of saying *selflessness.* In Mark 10:45 we read, "For even the Son of Man did not come to be served, but to serve, and to give His life a ransom for many." When we live to serve, not to be served, this is selflessness.

Q. How is functional unity maintained?
A. It is maintained by mutual _____
in love.

4. Can we always maintain functional unity?

No. It takes *two* to experience functional unity, but so far as it depends on us, we are to live at peace with all men.

CENTRAL PASSAGE: If possible, so far as it depends on you, be at peace with all men. (Romans 12:18)

We cannot always maintain functional unity, because unity is a two-way street. Both parties must be willing to act biblically in order to maintain unity. When one party is not acting biblically, then Romans 12:18 comes into play: "If possible, so far as it depends on you, be at peace with all men." Because of the way some Christians act, it is not possible to be in harmony with them, but so far as it does depend on you, be at peace with them.

If the husband is not submissive to the needs of his wife, harmony in the relationship can break down. When the wife is not submissive to the authority of her husband, harmony can break down. The same is true with parents and children and with employers and employees.

Sometimes the one in authority will abuse the one under him, and in such cases the one in submission is sometimes free to obey God rather than man. For example, a husband may try to force his wife to do something that is unbiblical. When that is the case, the wife is no longer responsible to submit to her husband. She submits to God as the higher authority (Acts 5:29).

There are a number of common ways that unity in the Body of Christ is broken. The most obvious is when one person sins against the other. However, sometimes it is simply a matter of an honest difference of perspective over a matter that is not sin. William Blake once wrote, "Both read the Bible day and night, but Thou readest black where I read white." How true that is. Life is filled with honest differences of opinion. In this case, when authority and submission are not at stake, the parties can agree to disagree amiably rather than to go to war over their differences.

> Q. Can we always maintain functional unity?
> A. No. It takes _____ to experience functional unity, but so far as it depends on us, we are to live at peace with all men.

Conclusion

In the Upper Room with His disciples the night before His crucifixion, Jesus poured out His heart to the heavenly Father in prayer. Since this was the last time He would be meeting together with all His disciples, you would expect Him to spend His time on things He considered most important. The dominant theme in His prayer was for unity of Christians. He prayed:

> And for their sakes, I sanctify Myself, that they themselves also may be sanctified in truth. I do not ask in behalf of these alone, but for those also who believe in Me through their word; that they may all be one, even as Thou, Father, art in Me, and I in Thee, that they also may be in Us; that the world may believe that Thou didst send me. (John 17:19–21)

Think of the implications of that prayer! Jesus prayed that Christians might be united in oneness, even as Jesus and the

Father are united in oneness so that the world could believe that Jesus was sent from the Father, or that Jesus was, in fact, God. What this means is that if the world looks at the Church and sees that it is spiritually unified, the world will have a basis to conclude that Jesus is who He says He is . . . the Son of God. If the world looks at the Church and does not see it living in unity, then the world has a basis for concluding that Jesus is not the Son of God.

Now the world would be wrong in coming to that conclusion, but they would have a reason for doing so. That is why the issue of unity is so important. It provides a backdrop for evangelism that allows the message to be accepted as credible. Without it, Christians are stereotypically perceived as a bunch of infighting hypocrites, and as a result the world believes there really is no God.

This unity is not organizational unity. The National Council of Churches or the World Council of Churches or a denomination or any other organization is not the unity that is being prayed for here. It is spiritual unity of brothers and sisters who are united in Christ and living their lives with each other in a spirit of love, mutual servanthood, and mutual submission. As the saying goes, "In essentials, unity; in nonessentials, diversity; and in all things, charity."

Review

CENTRAL PASSAGE: Behold, how good and how pleasant it is / For brothers to dwell together in unity! (Psalm 133:1)

1. Q. What makes true unity possible?
   A. True unity already *exists* because we are one in Christ.

2. Q. How is functional unity established?
   A. It is established by common *beliefs*.

3. Q. How is functional unity maintained?
   A. It is maintained by mutual *submission* in love.

4. Q. Can we always maintain functional unity?
   A. No. It takes *two* to experience functional unity, but so far as it depends on us, we are to live at peace with all men.

Self-Test

1. Q. What makes true unity possible?
   A. True unity already _____ because we are one in Christ.

2. Q. How is functional unity established?
   A. It is established by common _____.

3. Q. How is functional unity maintained?
   A. It is maintained by mutual _____ in love.

4. Q. Can we always maintain functional unity?
   A. No. It takes _____ to experience functional unity, but so far as it depends on us, we are to live at peace with all men.

T W E L V E

MONEY

CENTRAL PASSAGE: Do not lay up for yourselves treasures upon earth, where moth and rust destroy, and where thieves break in and steal. But lay up for yourselves treasures in heaven, where neither moth nor rust destroys, and where thieves do not break in and steal; for where your treasure is, there will your heart be also.

Matthew 6:19–21

More is said of money in the Bible, particularly in the teachings of Jesus, than of many of the Bible doctrines we have heard so much about, including hell, the church, or salvation. So much is said about money because it is more than merely the stuff we need to buy food, clothing, and shelter. Money, the Bible says, is the root of all kinds of evil (1 Tim. 6:10). Why? Because money is the basis of *more*. When we want more of anything, money is usually one of the things that will help us get it. And because a desire for more lies at the very foundation of the fallen heart, so does the desire for money. When Jesus, as well as the authors of the Bible, speak of money, they are addressing, not merely a commodity we need for daily existence; they are addressing an attitude of the human heart.

1. What is money the test of?

Money is the test of our *values*.

CENTRAL PASSAGE: Do not be anxious then, saying, "What shall we eat?" or "What shall we drink?" or "With what shall we clothe ourselves?" For all these things the Gentiles eagerly seek; for your heavenly Father knows that you need all these things. But seek first His kingdom and His righteousness; and all these things shall be added to you. (Matthew 6:31–33)

From God's perspective, money is a test. God uses it to test where our values are . . . where our hearts are. If our hearts are fixed on things of this earth, we find ourselves pretty tight with our money. If our values are fixed on heaven, we find ourselves trying to find ways we can give money to eternal things. Open heart, open wallet. Closed wallet, closed heart.

Benjamin Franklin once said there is nothing in money that will satisfy a person. Whenever money satisfies one desire, it creates two or three more. Yet money is the one common denominator that seems to dominate us all. We think if we could just have a little more, we would be happy. It is a subtle and formidable trap. Like a duped donkey, we trot mindlessly after the carrot of happiness we will never catch.

The Scripture exhorts us to lay up treasures in heaven, not earth. If we are living for the things of this world, it will be very difficult for us to spend our hard-earned money on the things of the next world. Only as we live for the things of the next world are we willing to give our money for the things of the next world. To understand money, we must understand that, not only is it an essential commodity for everyday life, but it is also a barometer of our heart.

> Q. What is money the test of?
> A. Money is the test of our _____.

2. Why should we give our money away?

To *advance* the kingdom of Christ.

CENTRAL PASSAGE: Now this I say, he who sows sparingly shall also reap sparingly; and he who sows bountifully shall also reap bountifully. Let each one do just as he has purposed in his heart; not grudgingly or under compulsion; for God loves a cheerful giver. (2 Corinthians 9:6–7)

Mark Twain once recounted the time he went to hear a missionary speak about the "savages" he was ministering to. As the missionary detailed the pitiful plight of the people he was working with, Twain purposed to give some money at the end of the talk. As the missionary went on, the amount of money he considered went up and up in his mind. He was going to write a check for a substantial amount. But then the missionary went on and on. The amount began to come down in Twain's mind.

The missionary went on and on and on and on. And when the plate finally came around at the end, Twain claims that he took a dime out of it. Needless to say, this reflects an inadequate motivation for financial giving.

The Bible teaches that we should give a portion of our money away, not only to demonstrate our commitment to eternal values, but to further our spiritual endeavors. So giving money to spiritual causes is not an option if we want to be an obedient follower of Christ. Giving our money to the furthering of His kingdom is an obligation . . . a matter of obedience.

If we come to the point when we are willing to give our money to things that reflect eternal values, we have to ask ourselves how much money we should give. That seems to be between the person and the Lord. Paul said in 2 Corinthians 9:7, "Let each one do [give] just as he has purposed in his heart; not grudgingly or under compulsion, for God loves a cheerful giver." Yet what each person purposes to do should be "to the degree that God prospers the person." Paul wrote in 1 Corinthians 16:2, "On the first day of every week let each one of you put aside and save, as he may prosper."

How much of one's money to give to "eternal" causes seems to be an issue in which each person must be "fully convinced in his own mind" (Rom. 14:5). However, with the emphasis Scripture puts on giving, stressing that it is a barometer of the heart, the sincere Christian will order his or her lifestyle to give regularly and sacrificially to the work of God.

Q. Why should we give our money away?
A. To _____ the kingdom of Christ.

3. Who owns the rest of your money?

God owns it all, and we are to spend it all according to His proiorities.

CENTRAL PASSAGE: I urge you therefore, brethren, by the mercies of God, to present your bodies a living and holy sacrifice, acceptable to God, which is your spiritual service of worship. And do not be conformed to this world, but be transformed by the renewing of your mind, that you may prove what the will of God is, that which is good and acceptable and perfect. (Romans 12:1–2)

Jack Benny, a comedian who was very popular on television in the fifties, built a reputation in his comedic role for being profoundly stingy. In real life he was actually a very generous man, but in one of his skits he was walking along and a thug came up to him and said, "Your money or your life!" There was a long pause, and Benny did nothing. The robber said, "Well, what will it be?" Benny replied, "Don't rush me! I'm thinking about it!"

When it comes to how we will spend our money, we don't want to be rushed. We want to think about it. Many Christians who give money to ministry consider what remains as theirs to spend however they wish. As a result, American Christians typically pursue the Great American Dream with the remainder, just the way non-Christians do. However, how Christians spend the money they do not give to ministry is not up to them. We must not fall under the misimpression that the money we give to the Lord is His, and the money we keep is ours. Not so. All the money is the Lord's. It is just that we give some away specifically to fund His kingdom issues. The rest, however, we are responsible to spend in a way that reflects our commitment to Him and our obedience to all the biblical commands and principles.

Our first priority, of course, is our family, if we have one (1 Tim. 5:8); the priorities there are food, clothing, and shelter. Scripture teaches that if we have food, clothing, and shelter we should be content (Matt. 6:25–34). Whatever money one spends, he must do so justifying how it relates to the ministry God has given him and to his obedience to biblical commands and principles.

Scripture also teaches preparing for the future (Luke 14:28) and being willing to put off things we want now for the sake of things we will need in the future. All money is the Lord's, and we are responsible to spend it in a way that honors Him and coincides with all biblical commands and principles.

Q. Who owns the rest of your money?
A. _____ owns it all, and we are to spend it all according to His priorities.

4. Is it right to go into debt?

The Bible always *discourages* going into debt.

CENTRAL PASSAGE: The rich rules over the poor, / And the borrower becomes the lender's slave. (Proverbs 22:7)

A panhandler came up to an executive on the street in New York and said, "Hey, buddy, can you spare two dollars for a cup of coffee?" The executive replied, "Two dollars? Even in the best restaurant, a cup of coffee won't cost you more than one dollar." "Oh," said the panhandler, "in that case, won't you join me?"

Nowhere in the Bible does Scripture explicitly forbid going into debt. On the other hand, nowhere in the Bible does Scripture encourage debt or talk about it as anything other than a negative thing: "The rich rules over the poor, / And the borrower becomes the lender's slave" (Prov. 22:7). There are some who believe that Romans 13:8 prohibits debt: "Owe nothing to anyone except to love one another." However, others believe that, in context, this does not prohibit financial debt but rather teaches that you should be in subjection to others, rendering whatever is called for: tax, custom, fear, honor, love, etc. Certainly it teaches that if you have debt you should pay it off. It may even prohibit debt, but Bible teachers are divided on that matter.

It is very difficult for Americans to absorb the biblical teachings of debt because we are so conditioned in our society to accept debt as a way of living. It is so natural that many Christians employ debt as a way of life without ever questioning it.

There are several reasons, however, to discourage debt, beyond the fact that the Bible discourages it. First, there is no way to know for sure if you will be able to repay the debt (James 4:14–15).

Second, going into debt often preempts the Lord. Had a need or even a desire been prayed for, the Lord might have answered our prayer, giving us the thing. However, when we go into debt and buy it, we keep the Lord from meeting our needs, from blessing us, and at the same time we put ourselves in bondage to something we cannot afford. Debt can teach our children to trust in ourselves and our own ability to manipulate life's system, rather than to trust the Lord (Matt. 7:7–8).

Third, if we default we may dishonor the Lord's name among people who know we are Christians.

Fourth, debt encourages us to live on a standard of living that we simply cannot afford, and the day of reckoning can become very painful (Prov. 22:27).

Fifth, if we default we may endanger all our other possessions and no longer have the ability to meet our family's needs.

We could go on and on with the dangers of debt. Again, while the Bible does not explicitly forbid debt, it always discourages it and talks about it in negative tones. The Christian who wants to live with God's view of money will take a very conservative view of debt.

> Q. Is it right to go into debt?
> A. The Bible always _____ going into debt.

Conclusion

Such warnings are well heeded, even in things done for the Lord. Hudson Taylor, an early-American missionary, wrote, "If the Word taught me anything, it taught me to have no connection with debt. I could not think that God was poor, that He was short on resources, or unwilling to supply any want of whatever work was really His. It seemed to me that if there were lack of funds to carry on a work, then to that degree, in that special development, or at that time, it could not be the work of God" (*Hudson Taylor's Spiritual Secret,* p. 58).

We must keep money in its proper perspective. It is a commodity that, like anything else, must be kept under the Lordship of Christ. Whenever we allow money to become our master, we become its slave. Money is a great servant, but a terrible master.

Review

CENTRAL PASSAGE: Do not lay up for yourselves treasures upon earth, where moth and rust destroy, and where thieves break in and steal. But lay up for yourselves treasures in heaven, where neither moth nor rust destroys, and where thieves do not break in and steal; for where your treasure is, there will your heart be also. (Matthew 6:19–21)

1. Q. What is money the test of?
   A. Money is the test of our *values.*

2. Q. Why should we give our money away?
   A. To *advance* the kingdom of Christ.

3. Q. Who owns the rest of your money?
   A. *God* owns it all, and we are to spend it all according to His priorities.

4. Q. Is it right to go into debt?
   A. The Bible always *discourages* going into debt.

Self-Test

1. Q. What is money the test of?
   A. Money is the test of our _____.

2. Q. Why should we give our money away?
   A. To _____ the kingdom of Christ.

3. Q. Who owns the rest of your money?
   A. _____ owns it all, and we are to spend it all according to His priorities.

4. Q. Is it right to go into debt?
   A. The Bible always _____ going into debt.

THIRTEEN

SUFFERING

CENTRAL PASSAGE: Consider it all joy, my brethren, when you encounter various trials, knowing that the testing of your faith produces endurance. And let endurance have its perfect result, that you may be perfect and complete, lacking in nothing.

James 1:2–4

In the movie *The Hiding Place*, adapted from the book by the same name written by Corrie ten Boom, a scene is set in the Ravensbruck concentration camp in Germany. Corrie ten Boom and her sister Betsy are there, along with ten thousand other women, in horrible, degrading conditions. They are gathered with some of the women in the barracks, cold, hungry, and lice-ridden, and Betsy is leading a Bible class. One of the other women calls out derisively from her bunk and mocks their worship of God. They fall into conversation, and this woman says what so frequently is flung at Christians: "If your God is such a good God, why does He allow this kind of suffering?" Dramatically she tears off the bandages and old rags that bind her hands, displaying her broken, mangled fingers, and says, "I'm the first violinist of the symphony orchestra. Did your God will this?"

For a moment no one answers. Then Corrie steps to the side of her sister and says, "We can't answer that question. All we know is that our God came to this earth and became one of us, and He suffered with us and was crucified and died. And that he did it for love" (*Illustrations for Biblical Preaching*, p. 365).

Suffering is one of the great themes of the Bible. You can't read very far before you come across suffering, and it continues

128

throughout the Bible until the very end. Suffering is a colored thread woven generously throughout the fabric of Scripture. Those who claim that if you are living the Christian life properly you will not experience suffering are not reading the Bible at face value.

1. Why does life have so much suffering?

While the Bible gives some reasons, we do not know the ultimate reason and must wait until we reach *heaven* for the answer.

CENTRAL PASSAGE: For affliction does not come from the dust, / Neither does trouble sprout from the ground, / For a man is born for trouble, / As sparks fly upward. (Job 5:6–7)

Why do people suffer? That question can be answered on a number of different levels. On a practical level, you can find at least five reasons: First, we suffer because of spiritual warfare. In the first chapter of Job, Satan is given permission by God to cause Job to suffer. In the end, Job is doubly blessed for all his trouble, but he really went through the fire to get there. Nevertheless, spiritual warfare may explain some of the suffering we experience. Second, we suffer because of a natural cause-and-effect relationship with sin. We steal, we go to prison. We lie, we lose our job. We have a bad temper, we experience broken relationships. Much of our suffering is self-inflicted because of sin. Third, we suffer because, as God's children, we are chastened . . . spanked, if you will, by a loving God (Heb. 12:1–11) in order to bring our lives into closer conformity with the character of Christ. Fourth, when we do not respond to God's chastening hand in our lives, we may experience His stern judgment. Finally, we have to admit that we experience, or see, suffering that seems, from the human perspective, to have no redeeming value whatsoever.

But these rather "practical" answers to the question of human suffering do not get to the heart of the problem as it exists for many people.

One of the greatest conundrums (exceedingly difficult questions) of life is reconciling the existence of a good God with the suffering that exists in the world. The problem is stated, with many variations, in this way: If God is all good and if God is all powerful, then where does the evil come from? The implication is that either God is not all good, in which case He does not care that people suffer, or He is not all powerful and is not able to do anything about it.

This is possibly the single greatest philosophical deterrent to Christianity. There are many ways people ask the question. They could ask, "Why do the innocent suffer?" And the answer could be, "Because of the fall there are no innocent." Or they could ask, "Why do the righteous suffer?" And you could answer, "There are no righteous. All have sinned." But both of these queries beg the real issue: If God were to care about humans as much as compassionate humans care about other humans, He would try to do something about the suffering. So there are no innocent and there are no righteous, but still, have some compassion! There are many humans who would end all suffering if it were in their power. So if it is within God's power, why doesn't He do something about it? How can God sit up there in heaven and watch all this suffering, knowing He could do something about it?

Frankly, after all has been said and said again a different way, I don't believe we really know. I believe the answer lies hidden in the mysteries of God.

Rabbi Harold Kushner wrote a book entitled *When Bad Things Happen to Good People* (Avon Books, 1981) in which he asks some very good questions and shoots down most of the usual answers for why people suffer. However, since he does not accept the New Testament as Scripture, his answers leave the Christian feeling a little empty:

> How seriously would we take a person who said, "I have faith in Adolf Hitler . . . I can't explain why [he] did some of the things [he] did, but I can't believe [he] would have done it without a good reason." If a human artist or employer made children suffer so that something immensely impressive or valuable could come to pass, we would put him in prison. Why then should we excuse God for causing such undeserved pain, no matter how wonderful the ultimate result may be?

Of course, when you begin judging God by human standards you automatically get into trouble, but it doesn't change the fact that the problem of pain and suffering is a very difficult one to justify with the amount of information we have and with the limited wisdom and moral capacity we have. When you boil it all down, it seems to come to this: No matter what explanation you come up with to try to justify God and pain, if God knew that, by creating mankind, even one person would go to hell, or if He knew His creation would fall and suffer so dreadfully, why would He not be willing to forego creating? Would not a kind and compassionate human forego creating something if he or she knew it would create the pain and suffering that is in the world today?

I am not sure it is possible to really answer the question on the level that most people want it answered. We simply may not have enough information, intelligence, or moral capacity to understand. But the solution is not to limit God (believing He cannot do anything about it or that He doesn't care) nor to jettison God and say there is no good God. That solves one problem (reconciling how there could be a good God and pain in the world at the same time), but it creates a hundred others (Where did the world come from? How do you explain the good in the world? How do you explain Jesus?).

Yet throughout the Bible, suffering is held up, not as something that is an embarrassment to God but rather as a "given" in life for the Christian and non-Christian alike. The Bible is unapologetically filled with the reality of suffering for God's people. Clearly, God is not intimidated by the difficulty of reconciling suffering with His goodness. So our task is to search the Scriptures for God's point of view on the subject. The Bible presents God as all good and all powerful, and the Bible presents the reality of human suffering. We may not be able to justify it to someone who does not accept God in the first place, but to those who do, there are some answers that can be very comforting in the midst of pain.

Q. Why does life have so much suffering?
A. While the Bible gives some reasons, we do
   not know the ultimate reason and must wait
   until we reach _____ for the answer.

2. Where is God when it hurts?
He is *with* us, feeling the same pain we feel.

CENTRAL PASSAGE: For since He Himself was tempted in that which He has suffered, He is able to come to the aid of those who are tempted. (Hebrews 2:18)

Where is God when it hurts? Is He off in heaven hosting banquets for the saints who have preceded us, blissfully unaware of our suffering? Is He casting down platitudes to us such as "Hang in there. It will all be over soon, and then you, too, can join the great party in the sky"? Many people think so. Many people have a mental image of a distant and uninvolved God who is enjoying the pleasures of heaven while He expects us to slug it out on earth until we die. Such is not the case. Where is God when it hurts? There are several answers to that question.

First, God, in the form of Jesus, came to earth, lived the life of a man, suffered ultimate humiliation and rejection during His ministry, and was tortured. Then He suffered a terrible form of death, crucifixion. He knew what was coming, and in the Garden of Gethsemane, he "grieved, to the point of death" (Matt. 26:38). The emotional stress was so great that the capillaries in His skin broke and He sweat great "drops of blood"(Luke 22:44). On top of that, which was bad enough, He must have suffered some dreadful experience when, as a holy God, the sin of the world was placed on Him on the cross and He cried out, "My God, My God, why hast Thou forsaken Me?" (Mark 15:34). There is every reason to believe that Jesus has out-suffered us. True, there are prisoners of war who have been tortured for years at a time, and someone might make a case for the fact that some people have suffered more than Jesus did. Yet, when you add the fact that the holy God took sin on Himself, that adds a dimension that cannot be equated by a merely human experience.

Because of all that Jesus suffered, He has always had credibility with me. He suffered and died for my sin. Anyone who has ever suffered terribly can, in the midst of his suffering say, "Jesus suffered more than this, and I caused it. He suffered and died for my sin." That is part of what Paul meant, perhaps, when he talked about entering into the "fellowship of His sufferings" (Phil. 3:10). We gain some appreciation for the love of God when we suffer terribly and then make the connection that Jesus out-suffered us and did so because of the sin we committed. Each of us can say, "We killed Jesus," because He would have died for us had we been the only one to have sinned.

Now this same Jesus is in heaven interceding for us when we suffer (Heb. 7:25). That is one answer to "where is God when it hurts?"

There is a second answer. God in heaven hurts when we hurt. God, being all-knowing, has the capacity for ultimate empathy. Theologians say that God's omniscience (all-knowing capacity) means that He knows all things, both actual and possible. So, because God is also loving and compassionate, when He sees His children suffer, He suffers with them. He enters into their suffering with unbroken empathy, and He feels everything they feel. Jesus wept over the city of Jerusalem when it became clear that the Jews were going to reject Him. He wept again at the funeral of His friend Lazarus. God the Father, throughout the Old Testament, grieves over the sin and rebellion of Israel. In his book, *Bold Love,* Dan Allender writes,

> Empathy is the human reflection of the incarnation, or God with us. God not only feels what we feel, but in fact, enters our condition and our flesh in order to fully bear our reality. Human empathy does not take away sin, but it mirrors the incarnation in that we possess the ability to (remotely) enter the pain and joy of others. (See 1 John 4:12.)

Philip Yancey, in his book *Disappointment with God,* wrote, "What human parent has not experienced at least a pang of such remorse? A teenage son tears away in a fit of rebellion. 'I hate you!' he cries, fumbling for words that will cause the most pain. He seems bent on twisting a knife in the belly of his parents. That rejection is what God experienced not just from one child, but from the entire human race."

Where is God when it hurts? Jesus is in heaven, having come to earth to out-suffer us, and is now praying for us when we suffer. Where is God the Father? In heaven, yes, but because He is omnipresent (everywhere at once), He also lives in the hearts of each of His children, feeling what we feel and suffering what we suffer. And not only what we feel and suffer but what everyone on earth suffers. And not only for our generation but for all generations who preceded us and for all that will come after us. God suffers more than any human, because He enters the suffering of all humanity.

Therefore, while we do not know the ultimate answer as to why God allows suffering in humanity, it *must* be for some justifiable reason if He did not exempt Himself from it. People could hurl all kinds of accusations about the goodness of God if it were not for that one fact: He has not exempted Himself from the suffering of humanity.

> Q. Where is God when it hurts?
> A. He is _____ us, feeling the same pain we
>   feel.

3. How does God view our suffering?

He views it as a normal part of the human experience on earth and promises sufficient *grace* for it.

CENTRAL PASSAGE: For this finds favor, if for the sake of conscience toward God a man bears up under sorrows when suffering unjustly. . . . For you have been called for this purpose, since Christ also suffered for you, leaving you an example for you to follow in His steps. (1 Peter 2:19, 21)

Scripture makes it clear that we will suffer. In Acts chapter 5, after the apostles had been flogged for preaching Christ, "they went on their way from the presence of the Council, rejoicing that they had been considered worthy to suffer shame for His name" (v. 41). Anyone who determines to live righteously in Christ Jesus may suffer persecution (2 Tim. 3:12). Such suffering will never be in vain, the apostle Paul writes (Gal. 3:4), and in fact, this is in keeping with Christ's example. Perhaps the central passage in Scripture in this regard is 1 Peter 2:20–24:

> For what credit is there if, when you sin and are harshly treated, you endure it with patience? But if when you do what is right and suffer for it you patiently endure it, this finds favor with God. For you have been called for this purpose, since Christ also suffered for you, leaving you an example for you to follow in His steps, who committed no sin, nor was any deceit found in His mouth; and while being reviled, He did not revile in return; while suffering, He uttered no threats,

but kept entrusting Himself to Him who judges righteously; and He Himself bore our sins in His body on the cross, that we might die to sin and live to righteousness; for by His wounds you were healed.

Then the apostle Peter went on to add, in 3:8–9, "To sum up, let all be harmonious, sympathetic, brotherly, kindhearted, and humble in spirit; not returning evil for evil, or insult for insult, but giving a blessing instead; for you were called for the very purpose that you might inherit a blessing."

No, suffering is not considered abnormal by God, nor does God treat it as some embarrassing facet of His creation that He overlooked or lost control of. Rather, for reasons that transcend our knowledge or understanding or both, suffering is part of life, and God calls us to it and goes through it with us.

Peter mentions that it is of short duration (5:10), though it never seems short at the time. Paul echoes this by saying, "For I consider that the sufferings of this present time are not worthy to be compared with the glory that is to be revealed to us" (Rom. 8:18). And again, "For momentary, light affliction [Paul had been stoned, shipwrecked, beaten, flogged, etc.] is producing for us an eternal weight of glory far beyond all comparison, while we look not at the things which are seen, but at the things which are not seen; for the things which are seen are temporal, but the things which are not seen are eternal" (2 Cor. 4:17–18).

Last, but certainly not least, God has promised that His grace will be sufficient for the suffering that we endure. Grace while suffering is very much like knowing the will of God. We often only see it in retrospect. But Scripture has declared that "No temptation has overtaken you but such as is common to man; and God is faithful, who will not allow you to be tempted beyond what you are able, but with the temptation will provide the way of escape also, that you may be able to endure it" (1 Cor. 10:13).

Q. How does God view our suffering?
A. He views it as a normal part of the human experience on earth and promises sufficient _____ for it.

4. How can we endure suffering?
By *fleeing* to the arms of God.

CENTRAL PASSAGE: For we do not have a high priest who cannot sympathize with our weaknesses, but one who has been tempted in all things as we are, yet without sin. Let us therefore draw near with confidence to the throne of grace, that we may receive mercy and may find grace to help in time of need. (Hebrews 4:15–16)

There are no formulas for suffering. It all depends on how badly you are suffering and whether it is physical or emotional or spiritual, or a combination of all three. It all depends on circumstances. Dietrich Bonhoeffer, who suffered in a German concentration camp, once said, "It is infinitely easier to suffer publicly and honorably than apart and ignominiously." It depends on your personality. Some people don't want anyone to know they are suffering; others want everyone to know. But nevertheless, while there are many individualities about suffering, there are some commonalties that may be helpful, and they all boil down to "fleeing to the arms of God."

a. Lean on Jesus during your suffering. In Psalm 61, David prayed,

> Hear my cry, O God;
> Give heed to my prayer.
> From the end of the earth I call to Thee, when my
> heart is faint;
> Lead me to the rock that is higher than I.
> For Thou hast been a refuge for me,
> A tower of strength. . . .
> Let me dwell in Thy tent forever;
> Let me take refuge in the shelter of Thy wings.

Of course, much of this is metaphor, but the point is, go to God, go to Jesus in prayer. Read the Bible to find out how Jesus dealt with adversity. Read in all the Gospels the accounts of His suffering, particularly in the Garden of Gethsemane. Pray to Him who understands all that you are experiencing. Let your suffering drive you to spend time with Him, and arrange your priorities in life around times alone with God. Hebrews 4:14–16 says:

> Since then we have a great high priest who has passed
> through the heavens, Jesus the Son of God, let us hold fast
> our confession. For we do not have a high priest who cannot
> sympathize with our weakness, but one who has been tempted

in all things as we are, yet without sin. Let us therefore draw
near with confidence to the throne of grace, that we may
receive mercy and may find grace to help in time of need.

Draw near to Jesus. Pray to Him continuously for mercy and grace
to help in time of your need.

b. Take comfort in the presence of God. The Bible
says, "I will never leave you nor forsake you" (Heb. 13:5 NKJV).
The Bible says Jesus lives within us, God the Father lives within
us, the Holy Spirit lives within us. God is present with us. Knowing this, we can take comfort in the conscious realization that
God is with us at all times.

c. Pray. Of course, if you are doing the first two things you
will be praying, but it deserves to be highlighted. Prayer, continuous prayer, can be a solace and strength while suffering. When
you are suffering, there are few rules for praying. It is sometimes
helpful to imagine Jesus sitting in a chair in the room you are
in, and knowing that He is there; tell Him what you would like
to say to Him if He were there physically. He is there spiritually,
and such imagining can help you make more complete contact
with Him intellectually and emotionally. Someone has said that
asking for help is the truest prayer we can offer in times of trouble.

d. Read the Scriptures. Most people who suffer find the
Psalms absolutely indispensable during times of suffering. The
honesty, the candidness, the transparency of David and the other
writers of the Psalms in crying out to God for deliverance and
solace bring a hope and sustaining grace that few other passages
of Scripture can equal. The accounts of the suffering of Christ
also can be very precious during these times, as well as the passages in the book of Revelation, especially chapters 4, 5, 21, and
22, which talk about heaven.

e. Cultivate an eternal perspective. Of course, many
of these interrelate, but the cultivation of an eternal perspective
is essential in coping with suffering. Alexander Solzhenitsyn once
said that the only way to survive in prison is to abandon all expectations of this world and begin living for the next. There are
times when suffering is very much like being in prison, and the
only way to cope is to abandon all expectations of this world and
begin living for the next. That is really what we should already

have done, but we don't until God, in His severe mercy, brings us to that point.

Paul, who suffered so significantly during his life, has eloquently made this point in several passages:

> If then you have been raised up with Christ, keep seeking the things above, where Christ is, seated at the right hand of God. Set your mind on the things above, not on the things that are on earth. For you have died and your life is hidden with Christ in God. (Col. 3:1–3)

> Therefore do not lose heart, but though our outer man is decaying, yet our inner man is being renewed day by day. For momentary, light affliction is producing for us an eternal weight of glory far beyond all comparison, while we look not at the things which are seen, but at the things which are not seen; for the things which are seen are temporal, but the things which are not seen are eternal. (2 Cor. 4:16–18)

> For I consider that the sufferings of this present time are not worthy to be compared with the glory that is to be revealed to us. (Rom. 8:18)

Many people have suffered more than I have, but I have suffered enough to know that in the midst of agony it is sometimes difficult to draw emotional funding from the future. We want relief *now*. Nevertheless, the Holy Spirit is often able to use these passages to bring us comfort, often while we are still suffering, but also after the critical stage of the crisis.

f. Family members and/or friends are often a major source of the grace of God during suffering. It is often through other people that the grace of God comes to us most meaningfully on an emotional level. My wife has been an angel of mercy to me during times of suffering, as have close friends who demonstrated to me a level of commitment and friendship that I never dreamed of. Church members are also often a source of prayer and support that strengthen us and help us endure times of suffering.

> Q. How can we endure suffering?
> A. By _____ to the arms of God.

Conclusion

It is true that those who believe in a God who is at the same time all good and all powerful must explain the existence of pain. (And that is no easy thing!) But atheists must explain everything else. That is even harder.

It is so hard to reconcile the existence of pain and God. Why doesn't He intervene? Why doesn't He make it right? Of course, one day He will, but what about now?

That is, in essence, what is being asked in the Book of Job. But God doesn't answer it. Instead, he gives Job a recital of His power and greatness: "God reeled off natural phenomena—the solar system, constellations, thunderstorms, wild animals—that Job could not begin to explain. If you can't comprehend the visible world you live in, how dare you expect to comprehend a world you cannot even see?" (Philip Yancey, *Disappointment With God,* p. 237).

We don't know the answers to the questions we ask about pain. What we do know is that God did not exempt Himself from it, and He gives us the grace to endure it. In the process, if we allow Him to, He will use the very pain we would give anything to get away from to make us more like Christ, which is the one thing in the world we want more than anything. It is quite a paradox.

God wants us to believe in Him by faith and to love Him . . . to love Him for who He is, not for what we can get out of it when we love Him, as though He were a cosmic vending machine. Christians get cancer just as non-Christians do. On the other hand, in order to vindicate His goodness, he promises hundred-fold blessings in heaven. It will eventually pay. We have to believe that for now and get the reward later. "The kind of faith God values seems to develop best when everything fuzzes over, when God stays silent, when the fog rolls in" (Yancey, *Disappointment With God,* p. 204). The challenge, sometimes, is not, as some people might lead us to believe, to live so close to God that we hear Him speak and see Him work every day . . . but rather to be so committed to Him in faith that we follow Him even when we rarely see Him or hear Him. The challenge is that, when we are in such pain we can barely stand it, when we are fearful because we see no change on the horizon, when we are so desperate that we don't know what to do because we cannot help ourselves and God will not help us, to bow the knee to God and say, "Dear God, in spite of everything, I still believe in You. I still trust You."

Review

CENTRAL PASSAGE: Consider it all joy, my brethren, when you encounter various trials, knowing that the testing of your faith produces endurance. And let endurance have its perfect result, that you may be perfect and complete, lacking in nothing. (James 1:2–4)

1. Q. Why does life have so much suffering?
   A. While the Bible gives some reasons, we do not know the ultimate reason and must wait until we reach *heaven* for the answer.

2. Q. Where is God when it hurts?
   A. He is *with* us, feeling the same pain we feel.

3. Q. How does God view our suffering?
   A. He views it as a normal part of the human experience on earth and promises sufficient *grace* for it.

4. Q. How can we endure suffering?
   A. By *fleeing* to the arms of God.

Self-Test

1. Q. Why does life have so much suffering?
   A. While the Bible gives some reasons, we do not know the ultimate reason and must wait until we reach _____ for the answer.

2. Q. Where is God when it hurts?
   A. He is _____ us, feeling the same pain we feel.

3. Q. How does God view our suffering?
   A. He views it as a normal part of the human experience on earth and promises sufficient _____ for it.

4. Q. How can we endure suffering?
   A. By _____ to the arms of God.

FOURTEEN

SPIRITUAL TRANSFORMATION

CENTRAL PASSAGE: I urge you therefore, brethren, by the mercies of God, to present your bodies a living and holy sacrifice, acceptable to God, which is your spiritual service of worship. And do not be conformed to this world, but be transformed by the renewing of your mind, that you may prove what the will of God is, that which is good and acceptable and perfect.

Romans 12:1–2

Transformation is fairly common in fairy tales. We all know of the prince who, because of a curse placed on him by a witch, was changed into a frog and could only be changed back into a prince if a princess kissed him. And sure enough, it happened. *Poof!* Instant transformation from frog to prince with one little kiss.

In *Snow White and the Seven Dwarfs* Snow White is transformed from a coma-like sleep by the kiss of a handsome prince. And in *Beauty and the Beast* the beast is transformed by the love of a beautiful maiden.

Yes, in fairy tales, transformation is glorious, sudden, and complete. Unfortunately, life is not a fairy tale, and we do not experience such sudden and complete transformation in anything. When we become Christians, we enter a spiritual transformation process that, if not understood, can be uncertain and discouraging because it usually takes longer than we ever imagined, is less complete than we wish, and is continually uncertain from our human perspective.

The Bible upholds the spiritual transformation process, especially in the New Testament (though we do read of it in the

Old Testament and see an eloquent plea for it in Psalm 119), as a major theme that, if we understand, can help us have hope in God's plan for our lives and take courage, strength, and direction in the process.

1. How does one enter the spiritual transformation process?

By being *born again* as a spiritual infant.

CENTRAL PASSAGE: Jesus answered and said to him [Nicodemus] "Truly, truly, I say to you, unless one is born again, he cannot see the kingdom of God." Nicodemus said to Him, "How can a man be born when he is old? He cannot enter a second time into his mother's womb and be born, can he?" Jesus answered, "Truly, truly, I say to you, unless one is born of water and the Spirit, he cannot enter into the kingdom of God. That which is born of the flesh is flesh and that which is born of the Spirit is spirit. Do not marvel that I said to you, 'You must be born again.'" (John 3:3–7)

Everyone who becomes a Christian does so as a spiritual infant. He may hold a Ph.D. in nuclear physics, have great wealth, and be both brilliant and wise, but he still comes into the kingdom of God as an infant (see 1 Pet. 2:2). Before that time, he is spiritually dead (see Eph. 2:1–2), which means to be cut off from God . . . to be in an unreconciled state from God (2 Cor. 5:19).

Just as physical children are very vulnerable and need to be taken care of with great oversight, so the new believer is very vulnerable and must be taken care of with great oversight. The physical baby is protected, spoon-fed essential nourishment, cleaned up often from his many messes, and loved into a greater degree of strength and awareness. So should the new convert be.

> Q. How does one enter the spiritual transformation process?
> A. By being _____ _____ as a spiritual infant.

2. What is the second step in the spiritual transformation process?

To press on to spiritual *maturity*.

CENTRAL PASSAGE: Like newborn babes, long for the pure milk of the word, that by it you may grow in respect to salvation. (1 Peter 2:2)

Just as a spiritual newborn must be taken care of hand and foot in his early days, so he must move beyond that state of passivity and dependence or he will never grow to spiritual maturity. In the early days, he must be spoon-fed or he will not make it. After he has gained some strength and growth, he must stop being spoon-fed and begin to feed himself or he will not make it. Interesting paradox! Yet just as it is true physically, so it is true spiritually. The newborn spiritual infant must begin to feed himself spiritually. Peter wrote, "putting aside all malice and all guile and hypocrisy and envy and all slander, like newborn babes, long for the pure milk of the word, that by it you may grow in respect to salvation" (1 Pet. 2:1–2).

In Hebrews 5:12–14, the writer exhorts Christians who have been careless or lazy in their pursuit of spiritual growth:

> Though by this time you ought to be teachers, you have need again for someone to teach you the elementary principles of the oracles of God, and you have come to need milk and not solid food. For everyone who partakes only of milk is not accustomed to the word of righteousness, for he is a babe. But solid food is for the mature, who because of practice have their senses trained to discern good and evil.

What an interesting explanation! From this we learn that it is our responsibility to press on from drinking only milk (the simpler things of the Christian faith) to eating meat (the deeper things of the Christian faith). The way this is done, it is implied, is with a desire to do what is right and a spirit of ready obedience. The mature person is one who has had his senses "trained to discern good and evil." The careless one, the one who is lackadaisical or lazy, will never have his senses trained to discern good and evil and will, therefore, never grow to spiritual maturity.

So we learn that it is our obligation to press on to maturity as soon as we have gained the strength and insight to begin to feed ourselves from the Scripture. We must be willing to do what is right and have a spirit of ready obedience.

Q. What is the second step in the spiritual transformation process?

A. To press on to spiritual _____.

3. What is the goal of the spiritual transformation process?

The goal is Christlike *character.*

CENTRAL PASSAGE: "Teacher, which is the great commandment in the Law?" And [Jesus] said to him, "'You shall love the LORD your GOD with all your heart, and with all your soul, and with all your mind.' This is the great and foremost commandment. The second is like it, 'You shall love your neighbor as yourself.' On these two commandments depend the whole Law and the Prophets." (Matthew 22:36–41)

When one asks what the goal of the transformation process is, the answer is the character of Christ. In Galatians 4:19, the apostle Paul wrote: "My children, with whom I am again in labor until Christ is formed in you." The central characteristic of Christlikeness is love. The Bible says God is love (1 John 4:16) and that anyone who loves is born of God (1 John 4:7). In 1 Corinthians 13:13, we read, "But now abide faith, hope, love, these three; but the greatest of these is love."

The central characteristic of love is that love gives. In John 3:16, we read that "God so loved the world, that He gave His only begotten Son." In Ephesians 5:25, Paul wrote, "Husbands, love your wives, just as Christ also loved the church and gave Himself up for her." Love gives. The essence of God and heaven is selflessness. The essence of the devil and hell is selfishness.

When we become spiritually mature, the mark of that maturity is love . . . love of God and love of others. The mark of that love is giving. Giving oneself to God in obedience from the heart to His commands and giving of oneself to one's neighbor when that neighbor has a need the mature one is able to meet.

This love is described in 1 Corinthians 13:4–8:

> Love is patient, love is kind, and is not jealous; love does not brag and is not arrogant, does not act unbecomingly; it does not seek its own, is not provoked, does not take into account a wrong suffered, does not rejoice in unrighteousness, but rejoices with the truth; bears all things, believes all things, hopes all things, endures all things. Love never fails.

This love is part of the fruit of the spirit described in Galatians 5:22–23, "But the fruit of the Spirit is love, joy, peace, patience, kindness, goodness, faithfulness, gentleness, self-control." This passage shows us a broader perspective on the mature person, but even in this we see love heading the list as the overriding characteristic.

> Q. What is the goal of the spiritual transformation process?
> A. The goal is Christlike _____.

4. How does spiritual growth take place?

By a *cooperative* process between God and the Christian.

CENTRAL PASSAGE: So then, my beloved, just as you have always obeyed, not as in my presence only, but now much more in my absence, work out your salvation with fear and trembling; for it is God who is at work in you both to will and to work for His good pleasure. (Philippians 2:12–13)

Spiritual transformation takes place by God's work in man and His enabling man to respond to that work—the Holy Spirit prompting, man responding.

In this central passage, we see that obedience is the response we are to have to the working of God in us. This work of God includes illumining our minds to the truth of Scripture (1 Cor. 2:12–16), convicting us of sin (John 16:7–10), and giving us a desire for righteousness (Gal. 5:22–23). We grow as we respond in obedience from the heart (see Rom. 6:17) to what God shows us, convicts us about, and gives us a desire for. Our capacity to understand and do good increases, so God is able to show us more (Phil. 2:12–13), convict us of the more deeply rooted sin we did not even perceive before, and give us an even greater desire for righteousness. This is the process of spiritual transformation from birth to growth to maturity.

> Q. How does spiritual growth take place?
> A. By a _____ process between God and the Christian.

Conclusion

Change is hard in all areas. Change is hard. Consider this letter from Martin Van Buren to President Andrew Jackson:

January 31, 1829

President Jackson,

The canal system of this country is being threatened by
the spread of a new form of transportation known as railroads. The federal government must preserve the canals for
the following reasons.

One, if boats are supplanted by railroads, serious un-
employment will result. Captains, cooks, drivers, hostlers,
repairmen and lock tenders will be left without means of
livelihood not to mention the numerous farmers now em-
ployed in growing hay for horses.

Two, boat builders would suffer and towline, whip, and
harness makers would be left destitute.

Three, canal boats are absolutely essential to the defense of the United States. In the event of unexpected trouble
with England, the Erie Canal would be the only means by
which we would ever move the supplies so vital to waging
modern war.

As you may know, Mr. President, railroad carriages are
pulled at the enormous sped of 15 miles per hour by engines
which, in addition to endangering life and limb of passen-
gers, roar and snort their way through the countryside, setting
fire to crops, scaring the livestock and frightening women and
children. The Almighty certainly never intended that people
should travel at such breakneck speed.

> Sincerely yours,
> Martin Van Buren
> Governor of New York

(from *Illustrations for Biblical Preaching*, pp. 37–38)

Ah, yes. Change comes hard. But change we must. If we
do not change, if we do not cooperate with the Holy Spirit in
the spiritual transformation process, we will be pulling spiritual
barges instead of railroad cars in our life journey, moving slowly,
ineffectively, and being left needlessly behind.

Review

CENTRAL PASSAGE: I urge you therefore, brethren, by the mercies of God, to present your bodies a living and holy sacrifice, acceptable to God, which is your spiritual service of worship. And do not be conformed to this world, but be transformed by the renewing of your mind, that you may prove what the will of God is, that which is good and acceptable and perfect. (Romans 12:1–2)

1. Q. How does one enter the spiritual transformation process?
   A. By being *born again* as a spiritual infant.

2. Q. What is the second step in the spiritual transformation process?
   A. To press on to spiritual *maturity.*

3. Q. What is the goal of the spiritual transformation process?
   A. The goal is Christlike *character.*

4. Q. How does spiritual growth take place?
   A. By a *cooperative* process between God and the Christian.

Self-Test

1. Q. How does one enter the spiritual transformation process?
   A. By being _____ _____ as a spiritual infant.

2. Q. What is the second step in the spiritual transformation process?
   A. To press on to spiritual _____.

3. Q. What is the goal of the spiritual transformation process?
   A. The goal is Christlike _____.

4. Q. How does spiritual growth take place?
   A. By a _____ process between God and the Christian.

FIFTEEN

TRUE SPIRITUALITY

CENTRAL PASSAGE: But the fruit of the Spirit is love, joy, peace, patience, kindness, goodness, faithfulness, gentleness, self-control.

Galatians 5:22–23

I have a couple of friends who are professional illusionists. Some people call them magicians, but they are Christians and stress that they are *illusionists* as opposed to *magicians* because nothing they do has anything to do with magic. It is all illusion—sophisticated, visual trickery that anyone can do if he or she has the talent and works hard enough.

But even though it is only illusion, it is truly amazing. I have seen one of them slide silver dollars around on a table and make the coins appear and disappear even though his hands made no sudden or unusual motions. I have seen my friend's wife apparently hang horizontally in midair as he passed a metal hoop around her body to show that there are no props or wires holding her up. I have seen white doves appear from "nowhere" and little white poodles disappear before my very eyes.

They are very good, of course, and both have made a living as illusionists for many years. I don't know how they do most of their stuff, nor is there a ready explanation for it. If there were, they couldn't make a living doing their shows. However, I have learned a couple of things about some of the more basic "tricks" that illusionists do, and when you find out how it is done, it is truly disillusioning. You think, *How in the world could I have been so gullible? There is nothing to it!*

But for the more advanced stuff, even though it may be based on illusion, the mechanisms used are so sophisticated and the skill necessary to execute the illusion without being detected is so advanced that it makes these people true professionals. My mind has been boggled again and again because, while these people tell me it is only an illusion, I see what I have seen and can come up with no possible explanation.

Illusions in entertainment are fun. But all of us are illusionists at the game of life. That is, we appear to be one thing on the outside but, in reality, are another thing on the inside. Sometimes this is done out of insecurity. We act happy or cool or sophisticated at a party because we are insecure and want to put on a facade so we can maximize the likelihood that the other people will think well of us.

Other times illusions are done out of a premeditated decision to be dishonest. We have done something we don't want anyone else to know, so we lie or act in such a way as to give a lie to the appearance. Still other times we may simply not be in touch with ourselves enough to understand the games we play in life to get our way or be accepted by our peers or relate to our family.

Because we get away with this illusion-making some of the time (less often than we think), we fool ourselves into thinking we can trick God, play games with Him, and get away with it. A quick reality check brings into focus the fact that we cannot trick someone who can read our minds and who knows all things. Nevertheless, we persist. We think that by acting spiritually on the outside, we will convince others, as well as God, that we are spiritual on the inside.

But while we may trick others, we cannot trick God. As God's children, we must learn one of the basic lessons running throughout the Old and New Testament, and that is that true spirituality is internal, not external. Until we live with a conscious realization of that fact, we will subconsciously keep up a game with God on the outside while never getting "real" and serious with Him on the inside. It is only the inside reality that matters with God, so it is the inside reality we must cultivate.

1. What is true spirituality in the Old Testament?

Loving God with all your heart, soul, and mind.

CENTRAL PASSAGE: For Thou dost not delight in sacrifice, otherwise I would give it; / Thou art not pleased with burnt offering. / The sacrifices of God are a broken spirit; / A broken and a contrite heart, O God, Thou wilt not despise. (Psalm 51:16–17)

There is a significant emphasis on "externals" in the Old Testament. The Mosaic Law is one of the most comprehensive external systems ever seen by man. The Law required excruciating attention to externals. Animal sacrifice, of course, was central to the Mosaic Law. When you sacrificed an animal, you killed it and burned it on an altar. But according to the Mosaic Law you could not kill it just any old way and you could not burn it just any old way. Bear with me as I quote from Leviticus about just one of the many kinds of sacrifice:

> But if the offering is from the flock, of the sheep or of the goats, for a burnt offering, he shall offer it a male without defect. And he shall slay it on the side of the altar northward before the LORD, and Aaron's sons, the priests, shall sprinkle its blood around on the altar. He shall then cut it into its pieces with its head and its suet, and the priest shall arrange them on the wood which is on the fire that is on the altar. The entrails, however, and the legs he shall wash with water. And the priest shall offer all of it, and offer it up in smoke on the altar; it is a burnt offering, an offering by fire of a soothing aroma to the LORD. (Lev. 1:10–13)

And if it was a bull or a bird or grain it was entirely different. You might ask yourself, on a cursory reading, Why did the goat have to be killed on the north side of the altar? What did it matter which side of the altar it was killed on?

My point is this: You had to pay excruciating attention to externals in the Mosaic system. There were peace offerings, sin offerings, guilt offerings. The priests had to ceremonially cleanse themselves before they could offer sacrifices, which meant that they had to go through a carefully prescribed process of preparation before they dared to begin. There were laws governing what animals you could eat and what you couldn't, laws about motherhood, laws about religious observances and feasts, laws about morality, laws of restitution for wrongs committed against others, and on and on. One slipup, and you could be dead, depending on which law you violated.

With all this . . . all this attention to external detail in the Law . . . God was not concerned merely about the externals. He was concerned about internals. Only if you believed in God and desired to be obedient from your heart to all these laws because of your love for Him would you be pleasing to God in the Old Testament.

God wants one thing of all of us, His children: to love Him with all our heart and with all our soul and with all our might (see Deut. 6:5). That is what He wants. In 1 Samuel 16:7, we read, "God sees not as man sees, for man looks at the outward appearance, but the LORD looks at the heart." In 1 Chronicles 28:9, we read, "As for you, my son Solomon, know the God of your father, and serve Him with a whole heart and a willing mind; for the LORD searches all hearts, and understands every intent of the thoughts." David said,

> For Thou dost not delight in sacrifice, otherwise I would
>   give it;
> Thou art not pleased with burnt offering.
> The sacrifices of God are a broken spirit;
> A broken and a contrite heart, O God, Thou wilt not
>   despise. (Ps. 51:16–17)

Yes, it is true, as Solomon said, "The refining pot is for silver and the furnace for gold, / But the Lord tests hearts" (Prov. 17:3).

It is what is in the heart that interests the Lord. Yes, He commanded strict observance to the Law, but the Law was a tutor, to reveal in material form the spiritual realities that would come with the Messiah, the Savior of the world. And the point was, if you truly loved the Lord with all your heart and with all your soul and with all your mind, you would go to the considerable effort necessary to keep the Law. If you did not love God with your whole heart, you would eventually begin to play fast and loose with the Law. It is as Isaiah wrote: These people "honor Me with their lip service, / But they remove their hearts far from Me" (Isa. 29:13).

This is exactly what we see happening. Perhaps the clearest example of this is in the book of Malachi when God says to the priests of Israel, in effect, "you are to honor My name, but you despise My name." The priests ask, in mock innocence, "How have we despised Thy name?" (1:6). God answers, "You are presenting defiled food upon My altar" (1:7). The sacrificial animals were to be without blemish, but these priests were presenting blind, lame, and sick animals for offerings. This and other distortions of the Law were severely reprimanded by Malachi.

God says, "This is sin, and for this I will judge you." God is concerned about the externals only as they are a sincere reflection of a right heart.

The details of the Mosaic Law are tests. If you love God with all your heart, soul, and mind, you go to the effort of following the commandments. If you do not love God completely, you begin to get lax with the fulfillment of the details of the law.

> Q. What is true spirituality in the Old Testament?
>
> A. _____ God with all your heart, soul, and mind.

2. What did Jesus teach about true spirituality?

True spirituality is "loving God from the *inside* out," not just making an external show.

CENTRAL PASSAGE: "You shall love the LORD your God with all your heart, and with all your soul, and with all your mind." This is the great and foremost commandment. The second is like it, "You shall love your neighbor as yourself." On these two commandments depend the whole Law and the Prophets. (Matthew 22:37–40)

Jesus was equally unambiguous about the meaning of true spirituality. He "nailed" the Pharisees more than once because of their hypocrisy, which is saying one thing and doing another or doing the right thing but with the wrong motives. In Matthew 23 He pronounced on them a scathing series of seven woes because of their hypocrisy. For example, he said in verse 23, "Woe to you, scribes and Pharisees, hypocrites! For you tithe mint and dill and cummin, and have neglected the weightier provisions of the law; justice and mercy and faithfulness; but these are the things you should have done without neglecting the others."

No, Jesus did not mince words on the subject of true spirituality. The entire Sermon on the Mount (Matthew 5–7) is devoted to the teaching that God desires our hearts, not merely our external actions. Yes, external actions can be important but not without our hearts as the motivation.

In all generations, the way to God has been by faith. By believing in God and giving our heart to Him, we then become obedient from the heart to whatever He asks of us. But to be obedient to those external matters just so we look good to other men is useless to God.

True spirituality is loving God from the inside out, not merely conforming to a bunch of external obligations.

> Q. What did Jesus teach about true spirituality?
> A. True spirituality is "loving God from the _____ out," not just making an external show.

3. What did the apostles teach about true spirituality?

It is an outworking of our *relationship* with God, not merely observing religious practices.

CENTRAL PASSAGE: So then, my beloved, just as you have always obeyed, not as in my presence only, but now much more in my absence, work out your own salvation with fear and trembling; for it is God who is at work in you, both to will and to work for His good pleasure. (Philippians 2:12–13)

The apostles, as they wrote their epistles to the early church, emphasized a balance between the two extremes of false spirituality: legalism and license (another word for excessive freedom). James Packer, in his book *Rediscovering Holiness*, introduces it well:

> Scripture and experience warn us that here we have to steer our course between two opposite extremes of disaster. On the one hand, there is a legalistic hypocrisy of Pharisaism (God-serving outward actions proceeding from self-serving inward motives), and on the other hand there is the antinomian [ignoring proper rules of conduct] idiocy that rattles on about love and liberty, forgetting that the God-given law remains the standard of the God-honoring life. Both Pharisaism and antinomianism are ruinous. Scripture and experience warn us that all Christians are at all times more weak, frail, foolish, undiscerning, and more vulnerable to temptations than they

realize. None of us escape the attentions of the devil—that malicious marauder who constantly manipulates the seductions of the world and the flesh in order to lay us as low as he can.

True spirituality in the epistles is presented as that balance between the working of God within the heart and the response of man to that work. Perhaps the apostle Paul expressed it most succinctly in Philippians 2:12–13 when he wrote:

> So then, my beloved, just as you have always obeyed, not as in my presence only, but now much more in my absence, work out your own salvation with fear and trembling; for it is God who is at work in you, both to will and to work for His good pleasure.

This is a very helpful picture that becomes slightly clearer as we look at it backward. God creates in us a desire to will and work for His good pleasure. As a result, we are responsible to respond and obey. This is what Francis Schaeffer, in his book *True Spirituality*, called "active-passivity," a phrase he coined to describe true spirituality. God works in us to realize that we ought to do something or ought not to do something. Or He gives us a desire to do something or not do something. Then we respond to that inworking, and when we do, it makes us spiritually stronger and more mature and, therefore, more eligible for God to work even more in our life.

The apostles were faithful to the teaching of both the Old Testament and Jesus when they stressed that true spirituality is a walk of faith and obedience to God from the inside out.

Q. What did the apostles teach about true spirituality?

A. It is an outworking of our _____ with God, not merely observing religious practices.

4. How does true spirituality affect worship of God?

God wants people who will worship Him in *spirit* and in truth.

CENTRAL PASSAGE: God is spirit, and those who worship Him must worship in spirit and in truth. (John 4:24)

When Jesus was speaking with the woman at the well in John 4, she said, "Our fathers worshiped in this mountain, and you people say that in Jerusalem is the place where men ought to worship" (v. 20). Jesus said to her,

> Woman, believe Me, an hour is coming when neither in this mountain, nor in Jerusalem, shall you worship the Father. You worship that which you do not know; we worship that which we know, for salvation is from the Jews. But an hour is coming, and now is, when the true worshipers shall worship the Father in spirit and truth; for such people the Father seeks to be His worshipers. God is spirit, and those who worship Him must worship in spirit and in truth. (vv. 19–24)

The only worship that means anything to God is worship that comes from our heart. To attend church regularly but not truly worship God in our hearts misses the mark. To worship God on Sunday but not any other time of the week misses the mark. Such compartmentalized worship is not true worship; it misses the mark. To think that we please God by observing church traditions or by giving money or by being faithful to denominational rules or any other thing is a misunderstanding of what true worship is.

If we sing a hymn and don't mean it or don't even let the words go through our mind, we are not worshiping God in spirit. If we pray but don't really have our heart in gear, if we are just saying words, we are not worshiping God in spirit. If we give our money grudgingly, we are not worshiping God in spirit. If we are in church but wish we were on the golf course, we are not worshiping God in spirit. If we are going through any motions but don't mean them, we are not worshiping God in spirit and in truth.

On the other hand, if we sing a hymn and mean it, we are worshiping God in spirit. If we read a passage of Scripture or pray with our minds engaged, we are worshiping. If we give our money sincerely, with a desire for eternal values to be advanced with it, we are worshiping. It is all a matter of motivation, sincerity, and mental engagement. Because God is not interested in externals without proper internal perspective, we must worship God in spirit and truth. We must worship Him with our minds in gear. As we go through the helpful external rituals of hymn singing,

Bible reading, corporate prayer, etc., we must mean it. When we do, we will worship.

> Q. How does true spirituality affect worship of God?
>
> A. God wants people who will worship Him in _____ and in truth.

Conclusion

C. S. Lewis once said, "No clever arrangement of bad eggs will make a good omelet." And no clever arrangement of external religious activity will make a pleasing relationship with God. Just as you want earthly friends who are true friends, not just backslappers in public, so God wants true friends. He wants people who have genuine relationships with Him. Christianity is not a religion. It is a relationship, and when we try to turn it into a religion, it goes sour. It offends God, it frustrates us, and it leads others astray if they imitate us. Everybody loses.

Review

CENTRAL PASSAGE: But the fruit of the Spirit is love, peace, patience, kindness, goodness, faithfulness, gentleness, self-control. (Galatians 5:22–23)

1. Q. What is true spirituality in the Old Testament?
   A. *Loving* God with all your heart, soul, and mind.

2. Q. What did Jesus teach about true spirituality?
   A. True spirituality is "loving God from the *inside* out," not just making an external show.

3. Q. What did the apostles teach about true spirituality?
   A. It is an outworking of our *relationship* with God, not merely observing religious practices.

4. Q. How does true spirituality affect worship of God?
   A. God wants people who will worship Him in *spirit* and in truth.

Self-Test

1. Q. What is true spirituality in the Old Testament?
   A. _____ God with all your heart, soul, and mind.

2. Q. What did Jesus teach about true spirituality?
   A. True spirituality is "loving God from the _____ out," not just making an external show.

3. Q. What did the apostles teach about true spirituality?
   A. It is an outworking of our _____ with God, not merely observing religious practices.

4. Q. How does true spirituality affect worship of God?
   A. God wants people who will worship Him in _____ and in truth.

SIXTEEN

ETERNAL PERSPECTIVE

CENTRAL PASSAGE: For momentary, light affliction is producing for us an eternal weight of glory far beyond all comparison, while we look not at the things which are seen; for the things which are seen are temporal, but the things which are not seen are eternal.

2 Corinthians 4:17–18

A young missionary lady lamented to discover that she was expecting a baby. She and her husband were ministering in a very primitive location in Africa, where they lived in poverty conditions, and they already had five children. It is such a burden to have children on a primitive mission field. There is never enough money, always too much work, and parents must endure the heartbreak of having to send their children off to school. When this missionary learned she was going to have another baby, she rebelled against God. Her health was not good, and it seemed more than she could bear.

When it came time for her to deliver she was very weak and there were no doctors nearby. There was no one to leave the other children with, so her husband put them all in the car and drove them into a town where there was a good mission hospital. They stayed there until the baby was born.

When they returned to their house with the new baby, they learned that in the short days they had been away, the dreaded Mau Mau had come. They had murdered every white person in the entire area. The family would have been killed had they been home.

As the lady told the story, she hugged the little baby to her breast, tears flowing down her face. "This little darling was sent by God to save all our lives. Never again shall I rebel against His ways for our lives" (from Corrie ten Boom, *Tramp for the Lord,* 122).

Lessons such as this teach us the importance of an eternal perspective. When we set our eyes on circumstances instead of the promises of God, we always misinterpret things and make wrong decisions. Or we languish in emotional turmoil that is unnecessary. To thrive in the Christian life we must interpret everything in this life in light of the next life. We must live in this temporal world with an eternal perspective.

1. What happened to original creation?

It was irretrievably *contaminated* by sin with the fall of man.

CENTRAL PASSAGE: For I consider that the sufferings of this world are not worthy to be compared with the glory that is to be revealed to us. (Romans 8:18)

Life is hard. It is harder for some than for others, but life is hard. Many of us grew up on the original Walt Disney, where we got the impression that if we dreamed hard enough, our dreams could come true. In the movie *Pinocchio,* Jiminy Cricket sang, "When you wish upon a star, . . . your dreams come true." When we see other Disney movies such as *Cinderella, Snow White and the Seven Dwarfs,* and *Bambi,* we come to the conclusion that everything in life will work out the way we want it to if we are just good enough, work hard enough, and believe completely enough.

With few exceptions, adults realize that those movies do not present an accurate picture of real life. Still, deep down within us, we have the die-hard belief that life will be good to us if we are just good in return. We are left shocked, stunned, and hurt when it doesn't work out that way. The Bible presents a more accurate picture: The wicked often prosper, and the righteous often suffer in this life.

Why is this? Why is the world this way? How did things get so backward? To answer these questions, we have to go all the way back to original creation as recorded in the first two chapters of Genesis. After each of the first five days of creation, God reviewed what had been done and said that it was good. Then, on the sixth day, God created man and woman and said that it was very good. Then God blessed the seventh day and sanctified it because in it He rested from all He had created.

But that good creation was irretrievably contaminated by sin with the fall of man.

Q. What happened to original creation?
A. It was irretrievably _____ by
   sin with the fall of man.

2. Is this world our home?

No. Because of sin, it is *hostile* to us, and it will be destroyed.

CENTRAL PASSAGE: But the day of the Lord will come like a thief, in which the heavens will pass away with a roar and the elements will be destroyed with intense heat, and the earth and its works will be burned up. (2 Peter 3:10)

God's original creation was good; in fact, it was very good. But shortly after that, sin entered this creation and everything changed. Instead of being a perfect environment for man, it became imperfect. Instead of being friendly, it became hostile; instead of being controllable, it became uncontrollable; and instead of being the paradise God created for man, it became a battlefield on which the forces of good and evil battle for the souls of men.

God's plan includes destroying this creation and recreating a world in which there will be no sin, or the possibility of sin (see 2 Pet. 3:10 and Rev. 21:27). Until that time, each generation must call upon the grace of God to make it through the life that comes to them in this fallen world. But this world is no friend to man. This world, as the old spiritual song goes, is not our home. We are just passing through. That, in essence, is an eternal perspective . . . living life with the conscious realization that we are just passing through this world.

We were not created for this world as it exists now; it will be destroyed. But God will save us from that destruction and bring us into a world in which sin has been removed and will never be reintroduced. Therefore, we are not to live for the things of this world. We are not to live with the value system of this world. We are not to fix our hopes on the goals and dreams of this world. We are to live for another world . . . the next world, realizing that our task here is to proclaim this message to others so that God can use us to save them from this world's destruction.

This is very hard to do because this world is "seen," and the next world is "unseen." It is always easier to keep in touch with something we can see. That, however, is our great challenge and the essence of maintaining an eternal perspective in life. We live, not for this world, but for the next.

> Q. Is this world our home?
> A. No. Because of sin, it is _____ to us, and it will be destroyed.

3. Is a new world being planned?

A new world is being planned in which there will be no *sin*, no death, and no sorrow.

CENTRAL PASSAGE: And I saw a new heaven and a new earth; for the first heaven and the first earth passed away. (Revelation 21:1)

Christian scholars throughout the ages have differed in their interpretation of when the next world is going to be ushered in and what it is going to be like. There are key questions such as When is Christ coming back? What events must occur before He returns? How much of the Book of Revelation is to be interpreted historically and how much is to be interpreted prophetically? How much of the language is to be interpreted literally and how much figuratively?

While the specifics of what the next world is going to be like are unlike, the character of the new world is not left in doubt.

> And I saw a new heaven and a new earth; for the first heaven and the first earth passed away, and there is no longer any sea. And I saw the holy city, new Jerusalem, coming down out of heaven from God, made ready as a bride adorned for her husband. And I heard a loud voice from the throne, saying, "Behold the tabernacle of God is among men, and He shall dwell among them, and they shall be His people, and God Himself shall be among them, and He shall wipe away every tear from their eyes; and there shall no longer be any death; there shall no longer be any mourning, or crying, or pain; the first things have passed away." (Rev. 21:1–4)

Then the apostle John went on to write:

> And I saw no temple in [the New Jerusalem], for the Lord
> God, the Almighty, and the Lamb, are its temple. And the
> city has no need of the sun or of the moon to shine upon it,
> for the glory of God has illumined it, and its lamp is the
> Lamb. And the nations shall walk by its light, and the kings
> of the earth shall bring their glory into it. And in the day-
> time (for there shall be no night there) its gates shall never
> be closed; and they shall bring the glory and the honor of
> the nations into it; and nothing unclean and no one who
> practices abominations and lying, shall ever come into it, but
> only those whose names are written in the Lamb's book of
> life. (Rev. 21:22–27)

That, of course, includes all who have received Jesus as their personal Savior.

> There shall no longer be any curse; and the throne of God
> and of the Lamb shall be in it, and His bond-servants shall
> serve Him; and they shall see His face, and His name shall be
> on their foreheads. And there shall no longer be any night;
> and they shall not have need of the light of a lamp nor the
> light of the sun, because the Lord God shall illumine them;
> and they shall reign forever and ever. (Rev. 22:3–5)

How different this new world will be from the one we are
in: No sin. No death. No pain. No mourning. No disease. No
accidents. No unkindness. No loneliness. No broken relationships.
Nothing to break the peace, love, and joy. That is the world to
which we are traveling. We are just passing through this world.
If we put our hopes and dreams in this world, we will be bitterly
disappointed. If this world is the only thing we have to live for,
no wonder people are unhappy! No wonder they turn to drugs
or alcohol or sex or work to numb the pain.

The problem is that Christians, who have the hope of the
next world, have lost sight of it. They receive no emotional funding from the hope of it and are living for the same "this-world"
gratification as everyone else. Consequently, they are just as
unhappy, in all too many cases, as non-Christians are. The beginning point to turn this around is the cultivation of an eternal
perspective.

Q. Is a new world being planned?

A. A new world is being planned in which there will be no _____, no death, and no sorrow.

4. How are we to live in this world?

We are to live in this world in light of the *next* world.

CENTRAL PASSAGE: If then you have been raised up with Christ, keep seeking the things above, where Christ is, seated at the right hand of God. Set your mind on the things above, not on the things that are on earth. For you have died and your life is hidden with Christ in God. (Colossians 3:1–3)

We are instructed to live by remote control. That is, all the directions, all the commands, all the information comes from another place, unseen but real. We live "here," as though we were citizens of "there." Paul elaborates in 2 Corinthians 4:16–18: "Therefore, we do not lose heart, but though our outer man is decaying, yet our inner man is being renewed day by day. For momentary, light affliction is producing for us an eternal weight of glory far beyond all comparison, while we look not at the things which are seen, but at the things which are not seen; for the things which are seen are temporal, but the things which are not seen are eternal."

The "momentary, light affliction" of which Paul wrote included, for him, being beaten with rods, being stoned, shipwrecked, being in danger from rivers, robbers, countrymen, and Gentiles, being in danger in the city, in the wilderness, on the sea, in labor and hardships, through many sleepless nights, in hunger and thirst, and in cold and exposure (see 2 Cor. 11:25–28). Paul was willing to endure whatever this world brought to him, because he was pursuing the values of the next.

The values of this world include, of course, peace and prosperity. The values of the next world include proclaiming the name and manifesting the character of Jesus. So if we must sacrifice peace and prosperity in this world in order to proclaim the name and manifest the character of Jesus, it is not only reasonable and logical, it is absolutely necessary.

It is necessary because Jesus commands it. It is reasonable and logical because God promises to meet our true needs in this life and reward us for all service in the next life. We have everything to gain and nothing to lose. It is as C. S. Lewis wrote that if you shoot for the next world, you get this one thrown in. If you shoot for this world, you get neither.

Q. How are we to live in this world?
A. We are to live in this world in light of the _____ world.

Conclusion

If we maintain an eternal perspective it becomes much easier to put off the things we ought to be letting go of and reach for the things we ought to lay hold of. Values are everything. We invest our time, energy, and emotional attachment to those things we value. If we value the things of this world above the things of the next world, we will never be satisfied. Never. Having an eternal perspective on the things of this life is perhaps the single most important thing we can do to give ourselves balance in the ups and downs of life and to give ourselves an even emotional keel in the disappointments and frustrations that inevitably come.

Review

CENTRAL PASSAGE: For momentary, light affliction is producing for us an eternal weight of glory far beyond all comparison, while we look not at the things which are seen; for the things which are seen are temporal, but the things which are not seen are eternal. (2 Corinthians 4:17–18)

1. Q. What happened to original creation?
   A. It was irretrievably *contaminated* by sin with the fall of man.

2. Q. Is this world our home?
   A. No. Because of sin, it is *hostile* to us, and it will be destroyed.

3. Q. Is a new world being planned?
   A. A new world is being planned in which there will be no *sin*, no death, and no sorrow.

4. Q. How are we to live in this world?
   A. We are to live in this world in light of the *next* world.

Self-Test

1. Q. What happened to original creation?
   A. It was irretrievably _____ by sin with the fall
   of man.

2. Q. Is this world our home?
   A. No. Because of sin, it is _____ to us, and it will
   be destroyed.

3. Q. Is a new world being planned?
   A. A new world is being planned in which there will be no
   _____, no death, and no sorrow.

4. Q. How are we to live in this world?
   A. We are to live in this world in light of the _____ world.

SEVENTEEN

DIVINE DISCIPLINE

 **CENTRAL PASSAGE:** All discipline for the moment seems not to be joyful, but sorrowful; yet to those who have been trained by it, afterwards it yields the peaceful fruit of righteousness.

Hebrews 12:11

No matter how you look at it, we are living in an age of permissiveness. I know there are those in every generation who describe the current age as an age of permissiveness, but no rational person denies that this time it's true! From school curricula to social behavior to child rearing to sexual behavior, this is an age of permissiveness.

A doctor recently reported a story that illustrates that our generation is so permissive we don't even recognize our own personal permissiveness. A young, unmarried man came to him to get a test for AIDS. The man told the doctor he was nervous because he had had intimate relations with a young lady on their first date and later on had found out that *she* had been sexually promiscuous!

1. Is the Church in America permissive?

Yes. We live in a permissive age, and whatever affects society will ultimately affect the *Church*.

CENTRAL PASSAGE: Do not love the world, nor the things in the world. If anyone loves the world, the love of the Father is not in him. For all that is in the world, the lust of the flesh and the lust of the eyes, and the boastful pride of life, is not from the Father, but is from the world. And

166

the world is passing away, and also its lusts; but the one who does the will of God abides forever. (1 John 2:15–17)

Lamentably, whatever affects our society affects the Church. Why? Because the Church is made up of the same people who make up society. Our churches are attended by non-Christians as well as Christians encompassing the entire spectrum of spiritual maturity from very mature to terribly immature. Therefore, since not all people in the Church are "saints" and since even all the saints do not think, feel, or act saintly, the world will creep into the Church, no matter what we try to do about it.

Therefore, we have in America today a permissive church. There is very little distinction between the lifestyles of many Christians and those of the mainstream of American society. The statistics on several telling issues are not significantly different between the churched and the unchurched. For example, the divorce rate is essentially the same. So is the alcoholism rate. So are the incidences of abuse. The television, movies, and music that Christians watch and listen to are little different from those watched and listened to by non-Christians.

But it is not just the easily spotted social behavior that is troublesome. There are more subtle things. Materialism in the church is essentially the same as for the unchurched. Living for the "here and now," what we get angry at, what we get depressed about, what we laugh at . . . in all these areas, we see too little difference between the churched and the unchurched.

We could be legalistic and just shout, "Cut it out!" But that was done for the last twenty-five years or so before our permissive age was ushered in during the sixties, and it didn't work. So what will work? Perhaps helping people understand how much God loves us. He loves us so much that He will not allow us to live unholy lives without paying a price, just as any loving parent would not allow his or her child to play in some dangerous place or with some dangerous object without being disciplined. C. S. Lewis called it God's "severe mercy."

The Bible makes it clear that there is a price to be paid for unholy living. Galatians 6:7–8 says, "Do not be deceived, God is not mocked; for whatever a man sows, this he will also reap. For the one who sows to his own flesh shall from the flesh reap corruption, but the one who sows to the Spirit shall from the Spirit reap eternal life."

God loves us too much to allow us to engage in dangerous behavior without paying a price, and He loves us too much to allow us to go through life believing that people, possessions, and circumstances are the key to fulfillment and meaning in life, rather than God. Therefore, in a permissive age, we would expect to see a lot of pain and suffering in the lives of Christians, and that is exactly what we see.

Christians' lives are being pummeled and thrashed in this generation like never before. Christians are suffering, and their lives are being buffeted as never before. There are reasons why, and when we understand them it will encourage us to flee to the safety of holiness.

Q. Is the Church in America permissive?
A. Yes. We live in a permissive age, and whatever affects society will ultimately affect the
_____.

2. Are there cause-and-effect consequences of sin?

If we sin, we pay an *automatic* price.

CENTRAL PASSAGE: Do not be deceived, God is not mocked; for whatever a man sows, this he will also reap. (Galatians 6:7)

The first reason Christians in this generation are being so buffeted is because there is a cause-and-effect consequence of sin. That is, as we commit a given sin, or adopt a certain attitude or perspective, we experience automatic, pre-programmed consequences whether or not we are Christians.

The Book of Proverbs is full of cause-and-effect warnings and instructions. For example, "A gentle answer turns away wrath, / But a harsh word stirs up anger" (Prov. 15:1). That is cause and effect. If you use harsh words (cause) you will stir up anger (effect). Or:

> Can a man take fire in his bosom,
> And his clothes not be burned?
> Or can a man walk on hot coals,
> And his feet not be scorched?

> So is the one who goes in to his neighbor's wife;
> Whoever touches her will not go unpunished.
>
> (Prov. 6:27–29)

We see here that going in to your neighbor's wife (cause) will result in your getting "burned" and "scorched" (effect).

The Book of Proverbs is filled with advanced warning on the cause-and-effect consequences of sin, and that is only one book of the Bible. The Bible is packed with such information. When we don't know the Bible well enough to be warned by these teachings, or when we know them but ignore them, we borrow trouble, unnecessarily bringing it down on our own heads.

In the permissive generation in which we are living, we fall into both traps. First, we are not disciplined in studying the Bible for ourselves and digging deeply into its reservoir of wisdom. So we do many things out of ignorance. Second, because the Church is infected with the spirit of permissiveness, we often think that we can violate the Scriptures without paying a price. These two traps cause many in the Church today to suffer pain that is entirely avoidable simply by becoming better students of the Scripture and by taking the Scripture more seriously in terms of obedience.

The church in Corinth, to which the letters of 1 and 2 Corinthians were written, was a permissive church, and they paid a terrible price of personal and corporate consequences, many of them the cause-and-effect consequences of sin. The same is true for the church in America or any other church. God has created the world with spiritual laws that cannot be broken. We can only break ourselves against them.

Q. Are there cause-and-effect consequences of sin?
A. If we sin, we pay an _____ price.

3. Does God discipline His children for sin?

God loves us so much He will not allow us to live in sin without paying a *significant* price to turn us from sin.

CENTRAL PASSAGE: My son, do not regard lightly the discipline of the Lord, nor faint when you are reproved by Him; for those whom the Lord loves, He disciplines. (Hebrews 12:5–6)

A second reason Christians are being so buffeted is because God loves us. Just as a loving parent teaches his children and disciplines them if his instructions are ignored or disobeyed, so God does not allow His children to live in harmful or dangerous ways without disciplining them.

Loving earthly fathers discipline their children "as [seems] best to them" (Heb. 12:10), but our loving heavenly Father disciplines with infinite wisdom. And discipline is always "for our good, that we may share His holiness" (Heb. 12:10) for the purpose of training us so we can experience "the peaceful fruit of righteousness" (Heb. 12:11). God loves His children too much to allow them to involve themselves in self-destructive behavior without trying to correct that behavior or those attitudes.

> Q. Does God discipline His children for sin?
> A. God loves us so much He will not allow us
>   to live in sin without paying a _____
>   price to turn us from sin.

4. Does God judge His children for sin?

Not in the eternal sense as with non-Christians, but on earth, God may extract a *severe* penalty, even death, for flagrant, prolonged sin.

CENTRAL PASSAGE: I have decided to deliver such a one to Satan for the destruction of his flesh, that his spirit may be saved in the day of the Lord Jesus. (1 Corinthians 5:5)

God does not judge the Christian's sin or punish the Christian in the same sense that He punishes the non-Christian. When a non-Christian dies he is punished for his sin, and it is pure punishment. There is nothing corrective about it because it is too late to correct anything at that point. In that sense, God never judges the Christian. The pain God allows into the life of His children is for the purpose of getting them to repent . . . to change their behavior.

However, it is apparently possible for a Christian to get hardened to sin to the point that he is utterly unrepentant. When this happens, God may bring severe chastening in his life and even take his life, which could be considered a form of judgment since there is no possibility of correcting the behavior once a person's life has been taken. Nevertheless, the behavior is corrected when he is taken out of his "body of flesh" and is free for his redeemed spirit to serve the Lord without the encumbrance of his fallen body.

So does God judge His children? Well, no, not in the technical sense of causing them to pay the eternal price for their sin. But does He judge them by bringing irrevocable calamity into their lives? Yes, sometimes, under certain circumstances.

It is easy to get in over one's head in this subject, but some things about the Christian and sin become apparent in 1 Corinthians 5. Flagrant sin was going on in the Corinthian church, namely that someone was cohabiting with his father's wife. This is probably the son's stepmother. The church, rather than responding properly to it, had become arrogant about it in some way. We don't know how. Perhaps someone suggested that the church do something about it, and the church suggested to that someone that he mind his own business. Whatever the case, Paul stepped in and sharply rebuked the church for not dealing with the issue and said he (in what way we do not know, perhaps some use of his apostolic power) has decided to deliver the sinning person's body over to Satan for the destruction of his flesh. Again, we don't know what this means in specific circumstances. But we do know that the person was apparently given over to greater Satanic influence in such a way that his body would be destroyed. However, his soul was saved.

This idea is reinforced in 1 Timothy 1:18–20, which reads:

> This command I entrust to you, Timothy, my son, in accordance with the prophecies previously made concerning you, that by them you may fight the good fight, keeping faith and a good conscience, which some have rejected and suffered shipwreck in regard to their faith. Among these are Hymenaeus and Alexander, whom I have delivered over to Satan, so that they may be taught not to blaspheme.

Why would God do such a thing? As a holy God, there is apparently a limit to the flagrant sin He will tolerate in the lives of His children. As long as we are sorry about our sin and fighting, although imperfectly, as much as we can against it, wishing we could do better, God is very patient with us. But at the point when we simply give ourselves over to the sin, not only not fighting it any longer but reveling in it, God looks at the matter quite differently. We are then subject to the "believer's judgment" of God in our lives.

This judgment may be circumstantial, it may be the removal of protection from satanic forces, or it may be physical illness. In 1 Corinthians 11, we read of people who are abusing the Lord's Supper, being gluttonous at a ceremonial meal and getting drunk on the communion wine. This was a well-known practice. Paul rebukes them soundly for such flagrant, willful, public sin and says that because of this sin, "many among you are weak and sick, and a number sleep" (1 Cor. 11:30). Paul is saying a rather remarkable thing here. He is saying that because of their sin, apparently God has directly caused some of them to be weak, some to be sick, and some even to die.

John wrote in 1 John 5:16 that there is a sin leading to death, that it is possible to sin so badly and so long that God will take the person's life. Some of the Corinthians had sinned to this degree over their treatment of the Lord's Supper, and the one who was living with his stepmother was on the verge.

Interestingly, we apparently see this man having repented and Paul urging the church to restore him to fellowship (2 Cor. 2:5–11).

Does God judge His erring children? Yes, He does if we stop battling the sin in our lives and give ourselves over to it. At what point does He do so? We don't know. The examples we have in the Bible are pretty extreme: adultery, and gluttony and drunkenness at communion. We cannot say more than the Bible says, but we *can* say (and must say if we are to be fair to a permissive church) that the point can come.

Q. Does God judge His children for sin?
A. Not in the eternal sense as with non-Christians,
   but on earth, God may exact a _____
   penalty, even death, for flagrant, prolonged sin.

Conclusion

All of us will have our lives publicly scrutinized between this life and heaven. Saint Paul wrote, "For we must all appear before the judgment seat of Christ, that each one may be recompensed for his deeds in the body, according to what he has done, whether good or bad" (2 Cor. 5:10). But some of us could fall under His judgment here on earth if we give ourselves over to flagrant, willful sin.

Two points need to be emphasized: The first is that if a Christian is living in flagrant, ongoing sin or has little change in his life to suggest that a spiritual new birth took place, the Bible encourages that person to evaluate himself to be certain that he is "in the faith" (2 Cor. 13:5). Second Peter 1:10 says, "Therefore, brethren, be all the more diligent to make certain about His calling and choosing you." That is, if when you evaluate yourself you see the presence of ongoing sin or the absence of positive fruit, just go back through and make sure you are a Christian. You might want to have another Christian talk through the salvation passages from the Bible with you, and you may even want to pray to receive Christ even though you have gone through the motions before. The point is not to question your salvation if there is no reason to question it; but if you do question it, it is as simple as going back through the salvation passages in the Bible and making certain of your belief in and receiving of Jesus as your personal savior.

The second point is that God does not judge the person who still cares about his sin, feels bad about it, and wishes he could be free from it. To this child, God has great patience. He may discipline so that the person can partake of a greater degree of holiness (Heb. 12:10–11) but does not judge him with sickness, death, or satanic destruction of his body.

The person who cares that he sins should read Psalm 103:8–11 for encouragement:

> The LORD is compassionate and gracious,
> Slow to anger and abounding in lovingkindness.
> He will not always strive with us,
> Nor will He keep His anger forever.
> He has not dealt with us according to our sins,
> Nor rewarded us according to our iniquities.
> For as high as the heavens are above the earth,
> So great is His lovingkindness toward those who
>   fear Him.
> As far as the east is from the west,

> So far has He removed our transgressions from
> us.
> Just as a father has compassion on his children,
> So the LORD has compassion on those who fear
> Him.
> For He Himself knows our frame;
> He is mindful that we are but dust.

As we saw earlier, there are several things that may account for suffering and pain in our life: the cause-and-effect consequences of sin, the chastening hand of our loving heavenly Father, and the inexplicable sufferings that come from living in a fallen world. Finally, if we live in willful, prolonged, unrepentant sin, God may begin to bring severe discipline in our lives. But we must not get trapped into thinking that all the pain that comes into our lives is because God is mad at us and is punishing us for something we did or didn't do. We must not forget the first three explanations for suffering and put all our focus on the third.

It is a dreadful trick of the devil to get Christians to think that God is punishing them for their sin when He isn't. One woman wanted to know, after her husband died, if God were punishing her for not living a better Christian life. The answer is categorically "NO!" God doesn't directly cause one person to suffer for another person's sin. Sometimes that is part of the cause-and-effect result of sin, but not the direct working of God. Each person is held accountable for his own sin, but no one is held accountable for someone else's sin.

This woman had the weaknesses we all struggle with, but she was not willingly living in any sin the Holy Spirit had convicted her of. God does not exact a pound of flesh from you for every sin you commit. If you are not willingly harboring sin in your life, then don't get trapped into thinking God is getting you back for things you have done. God doesn't work that way. He does not "get even" with His children. I spoke one evening with a young wife who lay dying from cancer. She wanted to ask me an important question: "Is everything OK? Is God doing this because He is angry with me?" I was able to assure her that God was not angry with her. This was just one of the inexplicable examples of suffering that come from living in a fallen world. She died a few hours later, in peace.

The only time God directly brings severe circumstances into our lives is when we have turned our backs on Him and we have knowingly and willingly embraced sin with no thought of repenting.

Review

CENTRAL PASSAGE: All discipline for the moment seems not to be joyful, but sorrowful; yet to those who have been trained by it, afterwards it yields the peaceful fruit of righteousness. (Hebrews 12:11)

1. Q. Is the Church in America permissive?
   A. Yes. We live in a permissive age, and whatever affects society will ultimately affect the *Church.*

2. Q. Are there cause-and-effect consequences of sin?
   A. If we sin, we pay an *automatic* price.

3. Q. Does God discipline His children for sin?
   A. God loves us so much He will not allow us to live in sin without paying a *significant* price to turn us from the sin.

4. Q. Does God judge His children for sin?
   A. Not in the eternal sense as with non-Christians, but on earth, God may exact a *severe* penalty, even death, for flagrant, prolonged sin.

Self-Test

1. Q. Is the Church in America permissive?
   A. Yes. We live in a permissive age, and whatever affects society will ultimately affect the _____.

2. Q. What are the cause-and-effect consequences of sin?
   A. If we sin, we pay an _____ price.

3. Q. Does God discipline his children for sin?
   A. God loves us so much He will not allow us to live in sin without paying a _____ price to turn us from the sin.

4. Q. Does God judge His children for sin?
   A. Not in the eternal sense as with non-Christians, but on earth, God may exact a _____ penalty, even death, for flagrant, prolonged sin.

EIGHTEEN

DIVINE WARFARE

CENTRAL PASSAGE: For though we walk in the flesh, we do not war according to the flesh, for the weapons of our warfare are not of the flesh, but divinely powerful for the destruction of fortresses.

2 Corinthians 10:3–4

Life is a battle. It always has been, and it always will be. The battle began before Adam and Eve were formed in the Garden. The battle began when Satan, then called Lucifer, the "star of the morning, don of the dawn" (Isa. 14:12), rebelled against his Creator and hatched his own plan to become like God. When God created man, Satan was right there to deceive and to destroy. He won a major victory when Adam and Eve fell for his trick, and the battle has intensified ever since.

Perhaps some readers will remember Louis Armstrong, the gravel-voiced jazz trumpeter whose heyday was in the forties and fifties. He recorded a song entitled "It's a Wonderful World" that I heard when I was a child. I don't remember all the words, but he would sing about how this thing in his life was going great and that relationship was flowering. And after each thing would come the refrain, "it's a wonderful world."

At the time, I was an insecure, struggling teenager wondering why it wasn't such a wonderful world for me. So I decided I would set out to make it a wonderful world, and I became an overachiever. Driven to succeed, I thought I could control the things I needed to control in order to make it a wonderful world and that there was something inherently wrong with me if I didn't.

It wasn't until I had been a Christian for a number of years, passing through phases in which I felt there was something wrong with me as a Christian if my world wasn't a wonderful world, that I finally woke up to the fact that life is a struggle. It is a battlefield, not a dance floor. It's a war, not a waltz.

There are two key truths to understand at this point: (1) Life is a battle, and (2) We cannot win it. Ironically, when we accept these two truths, the stage is set for our victory. Until then, the stage is set for defeat.

1. Who can win the battle of life?

Only the *Lord* can win the battle.

CENTRAL PASSAGE: The horse is prepared for the day of battle, / But victory belongs to the LORD. (Proverbs 21:31)

Only God can win the battle we are in because, as Christians, we are in a lifelong spiritual battle. Nothing happens to us that does not have spiritual ramifications. Both God and Satan make sure that we do not act in a spiritual vacuum. God is always with us, causing "all things to work together for good to those who love God, to those who are called according to His purpose" (Rom. 8:28). At the same time, the forces of evil are constantly battling against us to try to deceive us and destroy us (Eph. 6:11–18). So life, for us, is a spiritual battle, not only on a personal level but also on a cosmic level in the sense that the forces of good and evil are waging an unseen war in which many times we get caught in the middle.

In the Old Testament, there are some highly unusual stories designed to demonstrate that God alone can win the battle that we are in. As it says in Romans 15:4, the things that were written in the Old Testament were "written for our instruction." So when we see these stories, they have spiritual lessons for us today.

For example, the crossing of the Red Sea (Exodus 14) is probably the most dramatic. God led the children of Israel out of Egypt to the west shore of the Red Sea. They had no army as yet so they were, in essence, unprotected. Pharaoh changed his mind about letting them leave Egypt and sent his army to recapture them. God held off the army by a great pillar of fire, then parted the Red Sea so the Israelites could cross over to the other side. Then the Red Sea came back together again, saving them from the Egyptian army. For a time, there was no hope on the horizon. There was no deliverance for them in human sight. Yet God broke through the human circumstances and delivered them. There is a lesson for us there: There may be no hope on the human horizon, but God is always there, capable of delivering us at an instantaneous and unexpected moment.

Other stories abound: Joshua at the city of Jericho, David and Goliath, Elijah and the prophets of Baal. David said, "Some boast in chariots, and some in horses; / But we will boast in the name of the LORD, our God" (Ps. 20:7). Solomon said, "The horse is prepared for the day of battle, / But victory belongs to the LORD" (Prov. 21:31). God's work is done, "'not by might nor by power, but by My Spirit,' says the LORD of hosts" (Zech. 4:6).

While the circumstances in the New Testament are very different, the lesson is the same. Life is a battle, and the Lord must win it. For us to trust in our own resources is to go down in defeat. The apostle Paul stated this outright when he said:

> For our struggle is not against flesh and blood, but against the rulers, against the powers, against the world forces of this darkness, against the spiritual forces of wickedness in the heavenly places. Therefore, take up the full armor of God, that you may be able to resist in the evil day. (Eph. 6:13).

And again:

> For though we walk in the flesh, we do not war according to the flesh, for the weapons of our warfare are not of the flesh, but divinely powerful for the destruction of fortresses. (2 Cor. 10:3–4)

In the Old Testament, the battles were physical. The enemies were human. Today the battles are spiritual, and the enemies are spiritual forces of darkness. But the lesson is the same. The principle is the same. Only God can give the victory. You cannot put out fires with a floodlight. You cannot stop a flood with a flamethrower. And you cannot stop spiritual enemies with physical weapons.

Q. Who can win the battle of life?
A. Only the _____ can win the battle.

2. What does the Bible tell us about our efforts?

We are not to "take the law into our own *hands.*"

CENTRAL PASSAGE: For you have been called for this purpose, since Christ also suffered for you, leaving you an example for you to follow in His steps, who committed no sin, nor was any deceit found in His mouth; and while being reviled, He did not revile in return; while suffering, He uttered no threats, but kept entrusting Himself to Him who judges righteously. (1 Peter 2:21–23)

The Bible makes it very clear that we are to let God win our battles for us. It is not that we should be passive, as we shall see in section 4 of this chapter. But we must not assume responsibility for victory. We must not, as they used to say in the Old West, "take the law into our own hands." There will be many injustices in the spiritual battle of life. We will be treated unfairly, unjustly, and unkindly as we learn that deliverance comes from God, not from our own self efforts. Through his marvelous character Robinson Crusoe, author Daniel Defoe said, "God will often deliver us in a manner that seems, initially, to bring about our destruction." How true. There will be times when we think that, not only is the enemy attacking us but God, too, is either attacking or neglecting us. John Newton, the author of "Amazing Grace," said it as well as I have ever heard it said:

> I asked the Lord that I might grow
> In faith, and love, and every grace,
> Might more of his salvation know
> And seek more earnestly his face.
> 'Twas he who taught me thus to pray,
> And he, I trust, has answered prayer;
> But it has been in such a way
> As almost drove me to despair.
> I hoped that in some favored hour
> At once he'd answer my request,
> And by his love's constraining power
> Subdue my sins, and give me rest.
> Instead of this, he made me feel
> The hidden evil of my heart,
> And let the angry powers of hell
> Assault my soul in every part.
> Yea, more, with his own hand he seemed

> Intent to aggravate my woe,
> Crossed all the fair designs I schemed,
> Blasted my gourds, and laid me low.
> "Lord, why this?" I trembling cried,
> "Wilt Thou pursue thy worm to death?"
> "'Tis in this way," the Lord replied.
> "I answer prayer for grace and faith.
> These inward trials I employ
> From self and pride to get Thee free,
> And break thy schemes of earthly joy,
> That thou mayest seek thy all in me."

God has not abandoned us in those dark moments when heaven seems sealed in brass and God seems to be on the other side, unaware and unconcerned about our pain. He is still there. He still sees. He still cares. He is still the One who must deliver us, and we must still act accordingly. We are not to assume responsibility for the outcome of life's battles. Romans 12:17–21 reads:

> Never pay back evil for evil to anyone. Respect what is right in the sight of all men. If possible, so far as it depends on you, be at peace with all men. Never take your own revenge, beloved, but leave room for the wrath of God, for it is written, "Vengeance is Mine, I will repay," says the Lord. "But if your enemy is hungry, feed him, and if he is thirsty, give him a drink; for in so doing you will heap burning coals upon his head. Do not be overcome by evil, but overcome evil with good."

We are not to take revenge. But listen! There is more. When Jesus was teaching in the Sermon on the Mount, He said:

> You have heard it said, "An eye for an eye, and a tooth for a tooth." But I say to you, do not resist him who is evil; but whoever slaps you on your right cheek, turn to him the other also. And if anyone wants to sue you, and take your shirt, let him have your coat also. And whoever shall force you to go one mile, go with him two. (Matt. 5:38–41)

As Jesus' disciples exclaimed at another of His teachings, "Lord, increase our faith!"

The apostle Paul wrote in his first letter to the Corinthian church:

Does any one of you, when he has a case against his neighbor, dare to go to law before the unrighteous, and not before the saints? Or do you not know that the saints will judge the world? And if the world is judged by you, are you not competent to constitute the smallest law courts? Do you not know that we shall judge angels? How much more, matters of this life? If then you have law courts dealing with matters of this life, do you appoint them as judges who are of no account in the church? I say this to your shame. Is it so, that there is not among you one wise man who will be able to decide between his brethren, but brother goes to law with brother, and that before unbelievers? Actually, then, it is already a defeat for you, that you have lawsuits with one another. Why not rather be wronged? Why not rather be defrauded? On the contrary, you yourselves wrong and defraud, and that your brethren. (1 Cor. 6:1–8)

But that is not all. In fact, we are only getting warmed up. When you compile the passages they become overwhelming. In addition, Paul wrote, in Philippians 2:3–4, "Do nothing from selfishness or empty conceit, but with humility of mind let each of you regard one another as more important than himself; do not merely look out for your own personal interests, but also for the interests of others."

Finally, though it is by no means the last passage on this subject in the Bible, we see the apostle Peter instructing:

For this finds favor, if for the sake of conscience toward God a man bears up under sorrows when suffering unjustly. For what credit is there if, when you sin and are harshly treated, you endure it with patience? But if when you do what is right and suffer for it you patiently endure it, this finds favor with God. For you have been called for this purpose, since Christ also suffered for you, leaving you an example for you to follow in His steps, who committed no sin, nor was any deceit found in His mouth; and while being reviled, He did not revile in return; while suffering, He uttered no threats, but kept entrusting Himself to Him who judges righteously. . . . To sum up, let all be harmonious, sympathetic, brotherly, kindhearted, and humble in spirit; not returning evil for evil, or insult for insult, but giving a blessing instead; for you were called for the very purpose that you might inherit a blessing. (1 Pet. 2:19–23 and 4:8–9)

These passages make it clear that we are not to "take the law into our own hands" when we are wronged, but to trust in the Lord to vindicate us. That may not be until we get to heaven, but the Scriptures teach us to let God fight our battles for us.

> Q. What does the Bible tell us about our efforts?
> A. We are not to "take the law into our own
> _____."

3. Who or what are our enemies?

Our enemies are the world, the flesh, and the *devil*.

CENTRAL PASSAGE: We are destroying speculations and every lofty thing raised up against the knowledge of God, and we are taking every thought captive to the obedience of Christ. (2 Corinthians 10:5)

In the great battle we're in, there are three enemies: the world (see John 15:19), the flesh (see Rom. 7:18), and the devil (see 1 Pet. 5:8). Let's look at each enemy and see what the Scripture teaches us about each.

The word *world* is translated from the Greek word *cosmos*, which means "the present order and arrangement of things." The world, since the fall, has been the domain of, and under the control of, the devil. As a result, it is seen in the Scriptures as an evil place that has a very negative influence on Christians. It is not that everything in the world is bad, but bad things, along with some good things, are in the world and therefore the world cannot be trusted or lived for.

The apostle John, in his first letter, wrote, "The whole world lies in the power of the evil one," and:

> Do not love the world, nor the things in the world. If anyone loves the world, the love of the Father is not in him. For all that is in the world, the lust of the flesh and the lust of the eyes and the boastful pride of life, is not from the Father, but is from the world. And the world is passing away, and also its lusts; but the one who does the will of God abides forever. (1 John 5:19 and 2:15–17)

So we see from this that the world is an enemy of the Christian. It will lure the Christian to sin; to be a friend of the world is to be an enemy of God.

Our second enemy is the *flesh*. It is a difficult word to define. It has to do, not with our skin and bones, but with a power of sinfulness that resides within the unregenerate physical body of men. Paul said in Romans 7:18, "I know that nothing good dwells in me, that is, in my flesh; for the wishing is present in me, but the doing of the good is not." Paul stated that in his regenerate spirit, he wished to do good. But his flesh did not wish to do good. Rather, it waged war against the spirit (v. 23). That is why Paul said, in Romans 8:23, "we . . . groan within ourselves, waiting eagerly for our adoption as sons, the redemption of our body."

Our spirit has been redeemed, and nothing else needs to happen to our spirit before going to heaven. But our body will never make it. Our body is still corrupted by sin and still houses this "flesh," this pull to sin. So, according to this passage, when we get a new body, our redemption will be complete. We will then be able to stand before God untouched by sin in any way.

So the flesh is this pull to sin that remains with us even though we have been spiritually born again; this explains the civil war that rages within Christians that Paul describes in Romans 7. "On the one hand I myself with my mind am serving the law of God, but on the other, with my flesh, the law of sin" (v. 25).

The flesh is like a great Trojan horse; it is an enemy within. Even though our spirit longs to serve Christ, the flesh pulls us to sin. Paul's remedy is found in Romans 12:1–2.

> I urge you, therefore, brethren, by the mercies of God, to present your bodies a living and holy sacrifice, acceptable to God, which is your spiritual service of worship. And do not be conformed to this world, but be transformed by the renewing of your mind, that you may prove what the will of God is, that which is good and acceptable and perfect.

When we work this passage backward, we see that if we want to be a living demonstration that God's will is good and acceptable and perfect, we must be transformed. To be transformed, we must have our minds renewed. To have our minds renewed, we must present our bodies as living sacrifices. That is, we must live in complete obedience to Christ. That is the key to overcoming the enemy within, the flesh.

The third enemy we have is the devil. First Peter 5:8 says, "Your *adversary*, the devil, prowls about like a roaring lion." The devil is a deceiver. We read in Revelation 12:9 about "the serpent of old who is called the devil and Satan, who deceives the whole world." And he is a destroyer. In John 8:44, Jesus said:

> You are of your father the devil, and you want to do the desires of your father. He was a murderer from the beginning, and does not stand in the truth, because there is no truth in him. Whenever he speaks a lie, he speaks from his own nature; for he is a liar and the father of lies.

His goal is to do whatever he or his evil agents can do to subvert and destroy us. He deceives in order to destroy. He is our third, and perhaps, the greatest enemy of the three.

Q. Who or what are our enemies?
A. Our enemies are the world, the flesh, and the _____.

4. How can we be successful against our enemies?
By giving ourselves in complete *obedience* to God.

CENTRAL PASSAGE: "God is opposed to the proud, but gives grace to the humble." Submit therefore to God. Resist the devil and he will flee from you. Draw near to God and He will draw near to you. (James 4:6–8)

A primary enemy we must focus on is the world. We must be aware of our own capacity for sin and the lure of the world to sin. But Satan is a diabolical mastermind, commanding countless numbers of demons who have a specific strategy to use the world and the flesh as weapons against us. Therefore, while we must take biblical measures (see Rom. 12:1–2) to counteract the world and the flesh, the challenge is much greater against the devil. He has superior powers over mankind and has been at this a long time.

What does the Bible tell us about how we can let God fight this spiritual battle for us so we can win? If we try to fight it in our own strength, in our own wisdom and insight, and in our own way, we will lose every time. First, we must *be alert* to the *reality* of spiritual warfare. C. S. Lewis once said that there were two kinds of people who fell into two opposite and erroneous camps regarding the work of the devil: one who gave too much credit to Satan and one who didn't give enough. The trick, obviously, is to be balanced somewhere in the middle. But the Bible is unambiguous about the need to be alert. The apostle Peter wrote, "Be of sober spirit, be on the alert. Your adversary, the devil, prowls about like a roaring lion, seeking someone to devour" (1 Pet. 5:8). We tend to kid ourselves into thinking that we are not important enough for the devil to worry about. But apparently there are sufficient numbers of demons, all of whom do the bidding of Satan, that there are enough to go around for you and me.

Step number one in letting God fight your spiritual battles for you is to realize that you are *in* a spiritual battle and that you must rely on God's strength or you are already defeated. As Paul wrote:

> Finally, be strong *in the Lord,* and in the strength of *His might.* Put on the full *armor of God,* that you may be able to stand firm against the schemes of the devil. For our struggle is not against flesh and blood, but against the rulers, against the powers, against the world forces of this darkness, against the spiritual forces of wickedness in the heavenly places. Therefore, take up the full *armor of God,* that you may be able to resist in the evil day, and having done everything, to stand firm. (Eph. 6:10–13, italics mine).

It is God's strength that will enable us to stand firm, not our own.

Second, we must know the Scriptures well enough to use them in the battle against Satan (see Eph. 6:13, 17). If we don't know the Scriptures well enough, we must lean heavily on those who do until we mature to the point that we know them well enough to stand alone. In Matthew 4, we see Jesus having been led out into the wilderness where He was tempted by Satan. Each time He was tempted, He countered the temptation with Scripture. If that is the way Jesus battled Satan, how much more must you and I!

Third, we must cleanse our conscience. We will never have moral strength or moral authority until we do. The apostle Paul articulated his own perspective on the importance of a clear conscience in two different places in the book of Acts: "I have lived my life with a perfectly good conscience before God up to this day" (Acts 23:1) and, "I also do my best to maintain always a blameless conscience both before God and before men" (Acts 24:16). In 1 Timothy 1:5, he wrote, "The goal of our instruction is love from a pure heart and a good conscience and a sincere faith." So we see that a clear conscience is one of the goals of biblical instruction.

Later on in that same chapter, Paul wrote, "keeping faith and *a good conscience, which some have rejected and suffered shipwreck in regard to their faith.* Among these are Hymenaeus and Alexander, whom I have delivered over to Satan, so that they may be taught not to blaspheme" (1 Tim. 1:19, italics mine). Hymenaeus and Alexander suffered shipwreck in regard to their faith because they did not keep a good conscience. The same can happen to you and to me.

To gain a clear conscience, you must carve out sufficient time, and it could possibly take many hours, to ask the Holy Spirit to surface in your mind anyone you have offended or hurt and then others who have hurt or offended you. As the Holy Spirit does this, you determine to go to those whom you have hurt or offended and ask them to forgive you; also offer to provide any restitution that may be appropriate. This could easily be the hardest thing you have ever done in your life; if so, the prospect of keeping a clear conscience will be a deterrent to sin for you in the future because you will not want to go through this process again. Concerning those who have hurt or offended you, you forgive them. This may also be one of the hardest things you will ever do because you may find it extremely difficult to forgive someone who has hurt you grievously.

I wish I had enough time to personally share with you my own experience in going through this process so I could help you believe that I have some degree of understanding of how difficult this is on both counts. I understand some of the difficulty you may have with the process, but nothing changes the fact that it must be done if you are to have a perfectly clear conscience that will allow you to stand against the schemes of the devil and be victorious in the spiritual battle. You are battling God's way, and He is giving you the victory. An excellent resource for this is Kay Arthur's book and tape series, *Lord, Heal My Hurts.* A conscience that is unforgiving and harboring anger can lead to bitterness (Heb. 12:15) and make us vulnerable to our enemy, the devil (Eph. 4:26–27).

Another thing you must do to cleanse your conscience is to ask the Holy Spirit to surface in your mind anything you might have done or any activity you might have been involved in that could have opened a door for Satan to have influence in your life. This includes anything whatsoever to do with the occult, Satan, demons, parlor games, Ouija boards, séances, etc. Also, if there has been a history of any of this in your family, for some reason, it can open a door of influence for demons. Ask the Holy Spirit to bring to mind anything that might be in this category. Then repent of the activity, turn from it, ask the Lord to take back any ground Satan might have gained in your life because of it, and commit your life to shunning any such future involvement. If you think of things in this area, I encourage you to read Neil Anderson's book, *The Bondage Breaker.* It is a very thorough guide to this process.

The next thing you must do to be successful against your enemies is to cleanse your environment. If you possess anything that is a link to something you have just turned from, you must destroy it. It may be books, magazines, letters, videotapes, occult objects; they must be destroyed. We see the precedent for this in the Acts of the Apostles. Paul had been ministering in Ephesus, and God was performing extraordinary miracles by his hands. There was a large population of people in Ephesus who were involved in magic and sorcery. Paul's presence stirred up and agitated the demonic community there, and many of the magicians came to believe in Christ and gave their lives to Him. Then, as Acts 19:19 reads, "And many of those who practiced magic brought their books together and began burning them in the sight of all; and they counted up the price of them and found it fifty thousand pieces of silver."

These men who had been involved in the occult burned their books publicly. This had three effects. First, it confirmed in their own minds that there was no turning back. It was a bridge-burning incident that revealed the totality of their commitment to Christ. Second, it got the things out of their house so that Satan could not keep a foothold in their lives. Third, it became a public testimony to Christ.

Finally, to be successful against your enemies, you must give your life to God in total obedience. The apostle James wrote, "'God is opposed to the proud, but gives grace to the humble.' Submit therefore to God. Resist the devil and he will flee from you. Draw near to God and He will draw near to you" (4:6–8).

The apostle Peter reiterated this idea when he wrote, "Be of sober spirit, be on the alert. Your adversary, the devil, prowls about like a roaring lion, seeking someone to devour. But resist him, firm in your faith" (1 Pet. 5:8–9).

Paul said the same thing: "Therefore, take up the full armor of God, that you may be able to resist in the evil day, and having done everything, to stand firm" (Eph. 6:13). Trying to resist the devil without first submitting to God is foolhardy and risky (Acts 19:15–16). God has given us battlefield instructions, just as He gave them to Joshua at Jericho. If we humbly draw near to God and submit to His instructions, He gives grace to resist the devil and stand firm.

When we have followed God's instructions, being totally obedient to all we understand Him to be asking of us, we may stand firm against the devil. We may resist him in the power of Jesus, and when we do he must flee from us. We have it by the authority of the Word of God!

Q. How can we be successful against our enemies?

A. By giving ourselves in complete _____ to God.

Conclusion

Throughout the Bible, life is a war. In the Old Testament, we saw actual physical warfare, where the army of one nation went to war against the army of another nation. Much of what happened in the Old Testament on a physical level happened in the New Testament on a spiritual level. In the New Testament, the warfare was just as common and just as serious, but it was on a spiritual level: the kingdom of darkness against the kingdom of light. We are still caught in that war today. In the Old Testament, God wanted His children to understand that they did not have the natural resources to always be victorious. He did not want them to depend on themselves to win. He wanted them to rely on Him to fight their battles. God wanted them to realize that their sufficiency was in Him, not in themselves.

The same is true for us today. God wants us to understand that we do not have the natural means to emerge victorious from life's spiritual battles. He is our victory. He is our sufficiency. He wants us to rely on Him.

Review

CENTRAL PASSAGE: For though we walk in the flesh, we do not war according to the flesh, for the weapons of our warfare are not of the flesh, but divinely powerful for the destruction of fortresses. (2 Cor. 10:3–4)

1. Q. Who can win the battle of life?
   A. Only the *Lord* can win the battle.

2. Q. What does the Bible tell us about our efforts?
   A. We are not to "take the law into our own *hands.*"

3. Q. Who or what are our enemies?
   A. Our enemies are the world, the flesh, and the *devil.*

4. Q. How can we be successful against our enemies?
   A. By giving ourselves in complete *obedience* to God.

Self-Test

1. Q. Who can win the battle of life?
   A. Only the _____ can win the battle.

2. Q. What does the Bible tell us about our efforts?
   A. We are not to "take the law into our own _____."

3. Q. Who or what are our enemies?
   A. Our enemies are the world, the flesh, and the _____.

4. Q. How can we be successful against our enemies?
   A. By giving ourselves in complete _____ to God.

NINETEEN

EVANGELISM

 **CENTRAL PASSAGE:** All authority has been given to Me in heaven and on earth. Go therefore and make disciples of all the nations, baptizing them in the name of the Father and the Son and the Holy Spirit, teaching them to observe all that I commanded you; and lo, I am with you always, even to the end of the age.

Matthew 28:18–20

Evangelism, telling others about salvation in Jesus Christ, is part of the very heartbeat of God, and it is foundational to the story of the Bible. Throughout the Bible, God's people evangelized, and since the writing of the Bible, all people who have believed the Bible to be the Word of God have evangelized. If the message is true that man is lost, separated from God, and can be reconciled to Him through faith in Jesus Christ, it would take a very unreceptive heart not to think evangelism was important.

Paul said that to take the message of Christ to those who had not heard he had gladly endured being beaten, stoned, shipwrecked, in danger from rivers, robbers, the city, and the wilderness, and enduring labor and hardship, sleepless nights, hunger and thirst, cold and exposure (see 2 Cor. 11:25–27). The stories of missionaries after Paul's time reveal, in many cases, an equal zeal to take the message of Christ to those who had never heard:

> On November 10, 1871, in a remote area of Africa, newspaperman Henry M. Stanley met David Livingstone, a missionary of international fame who had been feared dead. Newspapers worldwide acclaimed the news! The encounter inspired Stanley to plead for missionaries: "Oh, that some

pious, practical missionary would come here! . . . What a field and harvest ripe for the sickle of civilization. . . . It is the practical Christian tutor who can teach people how to become Christians, cure their diseases, construct dwellings. . . . You need not fear to spend money on such a mission." (from *From Jerusalem to Irian Jaya*, Academic Books, 1983, p. 154).

That is the heart of a true missionary! And while missionary zeal is waning in the Western world, in the Third World, including many countries in Latin America and Asia, where the conversion rate is many times the birth rate, the missionary movement is gaining great force. Wherever the message of the Bible is revered, there will be evangelism.

1. When did evangelism begin?

In the heart of God *before* the world began.

CENTRAL PASSAGE: He chose us in Him before the foundation of the world, that we should be holy and blameless before Him. (Ephesians 1:4)

From the moment Adam and Eve "fell" in the Garden of Eden, ushering into the world all the pain, all the evil, all the suffering that has followed, from that very first moment, God has been occupied with redeeming lost mankind.

Why sin spoiled the original creation, we cannot now know. The answer lies in eternal mysteries that, if we ever fully understand, will not be until we reach heaven. But whatever the answer, the Bible leaves no doubt as to God's intent to save from the fall all those who will respond to Him and accept His invitation to salvation.

Revelation 13:8 speaks of the "Lamb slain from the foundation of the world" (NKJV) and Ephesians 1:4 speaks of God's having "[chosen] us in Him before the foundation of the world." Salvation of mankind was in the mind and heart of God even before the fall, a dominant issue from Genesis to Revelation. Therefore, God is evangelistic from Genesis to Revelation.

He offered salvation to Adam and Eve (see Gen. 3:21); He offered it to Cain and Abel (see Gen. 4:4–7). He offered it to Abraham, the father of all Jews (see Gen. 12:1–3), and He chose the nation of Israel, not to the exclusion of all the other people of the world, but in order to reach all the other people of the world. Psalm 67:1–2, 7 reads, "God be gracious to us and bless us, / And cause His face to shine upon us— / That Thy way may be known on the earth, / Thy salvation among all nations. . . . / God blesses us, / That all the ends of the earth may fear Him."

That is why God blessed Israel. That "all the ends of the earth might fear Him."

We see this principle exemplified when the queen of Sheba visited Solomon in 1 Kings 10. It was in the first part of Solomon's reign that the righteousness of the nation of Israel permitted God's greatest blessing, which lifted Israel to her greatest glory. When the queen of Sheba saw the glories of Jerusalem and the temple of God, she swooned ("there was no more spirit in her," 1 Kings 10:5) and then broke out in spontaneous eulogy to God: "Blessed be the Lord your God" (1 Kings 10:9). Note that she did not break out in spontaneous eulogy to Solomon, but to God. God's blessing on Israel was so obvious that it could not be attributed to man. It is the same principle as in Matthew 5:16, where Jesus instructs us to let our light shine before men in such a way that they may see our good works and glorify, *not us,* but our Father who is in heaven.

Yes, evangelism is in the heart of God, and that is demonstrated from the very beginning in the Old Testament.

Q. When did evangelism begin?
A. In the heart of God *before* the world began.

2. What did Jesus teach about evangelism?
That we are *responsible* to evangelize.

Jesus made it very clear from the outset that He was here for the purpose of evangelism. In Luke 19:10, Jesus said, "'For the Son of Man has come to seek and to save that which was lost.'" His entire message centered around the need for people to believe in Him and receive salvation. His parables focused on salvation. In Luke 15, Jesus gave three parables: one about a lost sheep, one about a lost coin, and one about a lost son. In each case the point of the parable was that God is not content until He has found that which was lost.

After Jesus chose His twelve disciples, He sent them out to proclaim the message of salvation. In Luke 10, He sent out seventy of His disciples with the commission: "The harvest is plentiful, but the laborers are few; therefore beseech the Lord of the harvest to send out laborers into His harvest" (v. 2).

In virtually every personal encounter Jesus had with individuals, His goal was to bring them to a point of decision about Him and about their sin. When He spoke to the woman at the well in John 4, He took the obvious and innocent subject of water and turned it into an occasion to evangelize.

Even as Jesus set His mind on the last thing He had to do, the issue was evangelism. He knew that unless He was willing to go through with the Father's plan for Him to die for the sins of the world, salvation would not be possible and evangelism would be fruitless. On the night of His arrest He went with His disciples to the Garden of Gethsemane on the Mount of Olives, where He prayed for the strength to go through with the plan. He asked three of His closest friends, Peter, James, and John, to be with Him while He prayed, telling them, "My soul is deeply grieved to the point of death" (Mark 14:34). He prayed to God the Father to please let Him out of this experience if there were some other way to accomplish what needed to be accomplished. Yet He ended up praying "not My will, but Thine be done" (Luke 22:42).

Finally, as He breathed His last on the cross, Jesus cried, "It is finished!" (John 19:30). What was finished? There were still sick to be healed, blind to be given sight, lame to be given strength. What was finished? The task of providing a way for man's sins to be forgiven. Jesus' own death in substitution for the death of all who would believe in Him and receive Him as their Savior (see John 1:12).

From beginning to end, Jesus focused on salvation. His whole life was centered around proclaiming the message of salvation by grace through faith in Him and then dying on the cross to give the message meaning.

After His crucifixion and resurrection, Jesus appeared to His disciples again and commissioned them for a task, the task that was to occupy them and all Christians until He returned, the task of taking the message of salvation to the world:

All authority has been given to Me in heaven and on earth. Go therefore and make disciples of all the nations, baptizing them in the name of the Father and the Son and the Holy Spirit, teaching them to observe all that I commanded you; and lo, I am with you always, even to the end of the age. (Matt. 28:18–20)

Q. What did Jesus teach about evangelism?
A. That we are all _____ to evangelize.

3. What did the early church believe about evangelism?

That they must *evangelize* at any cost.

CENTRAL PASSAGE: But you shall receive power when the Holy Spirit has come upon you; and you shall be My witnesses both in Jerusalem, and in all Judea and Samaria, and even to the remotest part of the earth. (Acts 1:8)

The disciples were thrown into confusion by the crucifixion of Jesus. While it seems that His plan should have been obvious to them by what He said while He was with them, for whatever reason it didn't sink in; they didn't understood the crucifixion and resurrection to be part of that plan. They were disoriented and frightened. But Jesus appeared to them after His resurrection, and they began to reflect upon and understand more of what He had said to them.

On the day Jesus ascended bodily into heaven, He was with His disciples on the Mount of Olives, just outside Jerusalem, and He gave them some final instructions. He told them that, while John had baptized with water, they would be baptized with the Holy Spirit soon (Acts 1:5). Then He reiterated the Great Commission He had given them in Matthew 28:18–20, only this time it was in more specific, strategic terms. He said that after the Holy Spirit had come upon them, they should be witnesses for Him, starting where they were (Jerusalem), expanding to the surrounding area (Judea and Samaria), and, in keeping with the Great Commandment, eventually going throughout the whole world. Then He ascended before their eyes into heaven (see Acts 1:8–9).

The disciples took up this mandate with great vigor, driving the religious leaders to distraction with their preaching. When they were commanded not to preach Jesus anymore their response was "we must obey God rather than men" (Acts 5:29). They were beaten and imprisoned (see Acts 12:4 and 16:23). No matter. The preaching and witnessing continued. Thousands came to know Christ through their evangelism (Acts 2:41). Indeed, they were following Jesus' mandate to be witnesses to Him in Jerusalem.

However, not much was being done in Judea and Samaria. Most of the Jews who had converted to Christ were apparently remaining in Jerusalem. Then a momentous event occurred. It was the stoning of Stephen. He had been detained by the religious authorities for preaching. When he refused to stop preaching and instead gave the officials a historical rundown of how bogus religious leaders had persecuted God's true spokesmen throughout history and had crucified Jesus, the Messiah, the religious authorities were so angered they stoned Stephen, making him the first Christian martyr (see Acts 6:7–7:60).

This kicked off a round of severe persecution as the religious leaders were inflamed to try to stamp out this movement of "The Way," as it was called. They began a search-and-destroy mission to find Christians and put them in prison. As a result, Christians fled the city into Judea and Samaria, taking the message of the gospel with them; in doing so they began fulfilling Christ's mandate to them.

Finally, Saul, a religious leader who was present at the stoning of Stephen, was converted to Christ and began making "missionary" trips to other parts of the Roman Empire to take the message of Christ to the Gentiles. Under his ministry and the ministry of others who were doing the same thing, Christianity spread like ripples from a rock dropped into a pond so that it was said of Jesus' followers that they had "turned the world upside down" with their teaching (see Acts 17:6 KJV).

Indeed, the early church believed in evangelism. The entire Book of Acts is the story of the spread of the gospel through Jesus' followers, and the message has continued to be passed down to this day.

> Q. What did the early church believe about
>   evangelism?
> A. That they must _____ at any cost.

4. What should the present-day church think about evangelism?

We should all accept the *mandate* to do the work of an evangelist.

CENTRAL PASSAGE: But you, be sober in all things, endure hardship, do the work of an evangelist, fulfill your ministry. (2 Timothy 4:5)

Of course the mandate for evangelism rests on the shoulders of all Christian generations. If evangelism is important to God, it must be important to us. The Great Commission given to Jesus' immediate followers logically passes down to succeeding generations. As long as there are those who have never heard the gospel of salvation by grace through faith in Jesus, those who have heard and accepted it are obligated to help pass on the message.

This can be done in several different ways. First, we can pray for the laborers and for the lost. Jesus said that the fields "are white for harvest" (John 4:35), and that "'The harvest is plentiful, but the workers are few. Therefore beseech the Lord of the harvest to send out workers into His harvest'" (Matt. 9:37–38). So we begin by asking the Lord to raise up people who will evangelize. In addition, we can pray specifically for individual evangelists. Paul often asked for people to pray for him and his ministry (see Eph. 6:19–20 and 2 Thess. 3:1–2).

Beyond that, we can pray for those who need to hear the message. Scripture teaches that no man can come unto Jesus unless the Father draws him (John 6:44). Each one must be convicted of his sin by the Holy Spirit (John 16:8). Prayer is the most important thing we can do in this regard because the people who need to hear the gospel are not blindfolded . . . they are blind. The apostle Paul wrote, "if our gospel is veiled, it is veiled to those who are perishing, in whose case the god of this world has blinded the minds of the unbelieving, that they might not see the light of the gospel of the glory of Christ, who is the image of God" (2 Cor. 4:3–4). It is not a matter of having "a word of prayer" before you get to work. Prayer *is* the work!

The second thing we can do, beyond prayer, is to give of our financial resources to support Christian ministries that further evangelism. How we use our checkbook is a surefire way of assessing our priorities (Matt. 6:24). If we look in the check register and see regular giving to Christian ministries, we know our priorities are in order. If we don't see regular giving, it means we still have growing to do in that area. We may not be able to give a lot of money. That isn't the issue. Jesus pointed out a woman who gave mere pennies to the temple treasury, and He said she gave out of her need; therefore, in His eyes she had given more than anyone else (Mark 12:41–44). There is not enough money in the world to pay to win the world to Christ. God wants our hearts, and one measure He uses to determine if He has our hearts is whether He also has our wallets. When we give, even if it is only a little, God is able to multiply our contributions, just as He multiplied the fish and the loaves when He fed the five thousand so that His work is accomplished. God doesn't need our money. He wants us. So we give as the Lord has prospered us. If He has prospered us a lot, we give a lot. If He has prospered us a little, we give a little. But the question is, Do we give? If we don't, growth is still needed in our spiritual lives.

The third thing we can do is live a life that attracts people to the gospel (see Matt. 5:16). God's primary goal for us after we become Christians is to work in our hearts to cause us to change into the character image of Jesus. As we do, people look at our lives, the only "Bible" some people will ever read, and they see all they will ever see of Jesus. Of course, none of us will show anyone Jesus perfectly. But if we live lives of continuous spiritual growth, people will look at us and desire to know Jesus because of what they see of Him in us.

The fourth thing we can do to help pass the message on is commit our lives to telling others about Christ. As we live a life of "relationship evangelism," we seek opportunities to tell others about Jesus. How we do this will vary with different individuals. The key is for each of us to ask the Lord how He wants us to be a witness and then be faithful to that.

I once heard of a unique approach by a man who had been used to lead many people to Christ. Someone asked him how it happened that so many people he talked to ended up trusting Christ. He said, "I only talk to people who are interested in spiritual things." The inquirer said, "Well, how do you know who is interested in spiritual things?" The man said, "I ask them." The inquirer said, "How do you ask them?" The man said, "I say, 'Are you interested in spiritual things?' If they say yes, we begin talking about spiritual things. If they say no, we don't." Using this unusual but rather obvious screening device, this man has led many, many people to Christ.

What a special approach! Each of us can also have an approach that is special to us. But each of us must be faithful to seek the mind of God as to how He wants us to be a witness for Him and then be faithful to how He leads us. Some people are specially gifted for evangelism (see Eph. 4:11). Others are not. But all are to do the work of an evangelist (see 2 Tim. 4:5).

I believe each person should get alone with God and say, "Dear Lord, you have commissioned each of us to go into our 'world' and preach the gospel. What, in light of the specific gifts, experiences, and relationships, etc., that You have given me, do You want me to do to further the Great Commission? I now accept the Great Commission as my Personal Commission and will do whatever You ask of me."

I believe when we ask the Lord He will give us His leading, His growth, and His blessing to be able to lead others to Christ. The key is not how many people we lead to Christ. The key is whether we are being obedient to the Great Commission.

> Q. What should the present-day church think
>   about evangelism?
> A. We should all accept the _____ to do
>   the work of an evangelist.

Conclusion

I used to minister with Walk Thru the Bible Ministries, an educational ministry to local churches teaching them an overview of the Old and New Testaments. One day a minister who was deeply burdened for evangelism challenged us that we were not presenting the gospel during our seminars. We explained that we were not an evangelistic ministry but a teaching ministry to people who were already Christians. The preacher wouldn't buy that answer. He said, "You have hundreds of people sitting before the teaching of God's Word for eight hours on a Saturday. Some of them are bound to be non-Christians. They can't sit through the teaching of the Word that long without some of them coming under conviction. There are bound to be people who want to become Christians in your seminars, and you are not giving them a chance!"

He seemed to have a valid point, so we incorporated a brief amount of time at the end of our seminars for people to come to Christ if they would like to. Frankly, we did it merely as an experiment, not expecting much. But in the next twelve months, five thousand people came to Christ through the Walk Thru seminars! That was more than a decade ago. Who knows how many people in the history of that "teaching" ministry have come to Christ since then? All because, at the prompting of an evangelist, we began asking.

A similar story is told of when Henry Ford purchased a large insurance policy. The Detroit newspapers blazoned the fact since the amount was so large and he was so prominent. When a friend of Ford's who was in the insurance business read the story he called Ford to see if it were true. Ford assured him it was. The friend said, "Well, why didn't you buy it from me?" Ford replied, "You never asked."

I believe we will see people in heaven we don't expect, and when we ask them why they didn't become Christians from talking to us they will say, "You never asked." We need to gain a boldness from a clear conscience and a conviction of the needs of the lost and begin asking. We may be surprised how many will say yes.

Review

CENTRAL PASSAGE: All authority has been given to Me in heaven and on earth. Go therefore and make disciples of all the nations, baptizing them in the name of the Father and the Son and the Holy Spirit, teaching them to observe all that I commanded you; and lo, I am with you always, even to the end of the age. (Matthew 28:18–20)

1. Q. When did evangelism begin?
   A. In the heart of God *before* the world began.

2. Q. What did Jesus teach about evangelism?
   A. That we are all *responsible* to evangelize.

3. Q. What did the early church believe about evangelism?
   A. That they must *evangelize* at any cost.

4. Q. What should the present-day church think about evangelism?
   A. We should all accept the *mandate* to do the work of an evangelist.

Self-Test

1. Q. When did evangelism begin?
   A. In the heart of God _____ the world began.

2. Q. What did Jesus teach about evangelism?
   A. That we are all _____ to evangelize.

3. Q. What did the early church believe about evangelism?
   A. That they must _____ at any cost.

4. Q. What should the present-day church think about evangelism?
   A. We should all accept the _____ to do the work of an evangelist.

TWENTY

DOING GOOD

CENTRAL PASSAGE: For we are His workmanship, created in Christ Jesus for good works, which God prepared beforehand, that we should walk in them.

Ephesians 2:10

The Rhodes Scholarship is one of the most prestigious academic scholarships available today. It was established by Cecil John Rhodes, who was a South African statesman and financier. He gained a vast fortune in gold and diamond mining and used part of his fortune upon his death to establish the famous scholarships.

Though he was fabulously wealthy, he was a sensitive and kind man. The story is told of a young man who was invited to dine with Rhodes in his lovely home; the man arrived by train too late to change and had to go immediately to Rhodes's house in his travel-stained clothes. He was deeply embarrassed to find all the other guests already gathered for dinner in full evening dress. After what seemed like a long time, Rhodes finally appeared in a shabby, old, blue suit. The young man later learned that when he arrived, Rhodes had been dressed in evening clothes and was about to welcome his guests. Told of the traveler's dilemma, Rhodes had at once returned to his bedroom and put on the old suit.

What an act of kindness; what a good thing to do! Doing good is not something that is widely and greatly admired today. In fact, the heroes of many of the modern movies and books are "anti-heroes," that is, bad people. Today the derogatory phrase, "goody two-shoes" is used to describe people who are bent on doing good. Admittedly, it sometimes has the connotation of hypocrisy, but not always. Sometimes, it is just a slam against a person who tries to do good.

However, the concept of doing good runs throughout the Bible. It starts in the first chapter of Genesis and ends in the last chapter of Revelation, with the words *good* and *goodness* occurring more than 570 times.

1. Where does goodness come from?

It is a reflection of the *character* of God.

CENTRAL PASSAGE: Beloved, do not imitate what is evil, but what is good. The one who does good is of God; the one who does evil has not seen God. (3 John 11)

Doing good reflects the character of God. It has been God's intention from the very beginning of creation to do good. After the first five days of creation God pronounced the results "good." After the sixth day of creation, which was the day He created Adam and Eve, He said it was "very good." Then He rested on the seventh day.

He chose Israel and promised to do good for her (see Num. 10:29). He gave Israel commandments to keep "for your own good" (Deut. 10:13). Everything God asks of us is for our own good because He wants to give something good to us and to keep some harm from us. Second Chronicles 7:3 says, "Truly [the Lord] is good, truly His lovingkindness is everlasting." David said in Psalm 119:68 that the Lord is good and that everything He does is good.

In the New Testament, Jesus calls Himself "the good shepherd" (John 10:14). The apostle Paul wrote in Romans 8:28, "all things work together for good to those who love God, to those who are called according to His purpose." Romans 12:1–2 teaches us that God's will is good and perfect. In Philippians 1:6 we read that "He who began a good work in you will perfect it until the day of Christ Jesus."

We might ask ourselves what it means to be good. The Bible does not define it, but the dictionary defines it as "having desirable properties, gratifying, enjoyable, beneficial, morally upright." So God has gone on record as saying that His original creation had desirable properties and was gratifying, enjoyable, beneficial, and morally upright.

In addition, He extends to His children a gratifying, enjoyable, beneficial, and morally upright experience and relationship with Him. He does this by giving us commands and instructions to follow and by providentially working in our lives.

The point is this: God is good, and when the Bible says that He intends to do good for His children, it means He intends to do something for His children that they will enjoy and benefit from . . . forever.

There are two extremes that must be avoided in understanding the goodness of God. First, it must be understood that God is not out to please only Himself with His creation, regardless of the impact on the creation. It is not that God is going to do with mankind what He chooses, even though that might not be good for mankind. The only way we can understand the goodness of God is to understand that what He is doing is desirable from His children's standpoint. God is not an engineer or a scientist fooling around with human toys for His own enjoyment. Otherwise He could hatch all kinds of sadistic schemes against His hapless children, plunging them into senseless misery purely for His own enjoyment, but this would not stand up to any known definition of goodness.

There are those who sometimes have a difficult time reconciling God's goodness with the pain and suffering in the world, especially when His children suffer. However, it would be wrong to assume that God's definition of goodness would allow Him to be sadistic toward His creation for His own hidden purpose or amusement.

The second extreme to be avoided is that, when we say God intends to do good for His children, this implies life will always be easy and pleasurable. We live in a fallen world in which the effects of sin have changed the original game plan. Just as a surgeon must sometimes hurt in order to heal, so God sometimes allows pain into our lives, then He uses it for a good purpose. Being a child of God is not like belonging to Santa Claus, where one can expect unbroken pleasure. God delivers us *through* the pain inherent in a fallen world but does not deliver us *from* it all.

The truth lies somewhere in between these two extremes, as we have seen. We can summarize it by saying that, in the end, all will be well even though some things in life will be difficult.

Suffering is part of the Christian experience. The first chapter of James and the entire book of 1 Peter teach us that unambiguously. But in the pain and through the life of sin into which we are all born God will work good in our lives. And in the end He will usher us into a life of unbroken bliss with Him as He does good for us forever.

Q. Where does goodness come from?
A. It is a reflection of the _____ of God.

2. What good are we to do?

We are to *reflect* the character of Jesus in all we do.

CENTRAL PASSAGE: And do not neglect doing good and sharing; for with such sacrifices God is pleased. (Hebrews 13:16)

If God is good and does good, and if we are to be like God, then we must do good. Jesus said in the Sermon on the Mount, "Let your light shine before men in such a way that they may see your good works, and glorify your Father who is in heaven" (Matt. 5:16). From the moment when we were born again (John 3:3), our "inner man" is holy and righteous, created in the likeness of God (see Romans 7 and Eph. 4:24). So our regenerate spirit is good, just as God is good. But in the mystery of spiritual life, the power of sin in the flesh and the susceptibility of the flesh to temptation and deceit by Satan causes us not to always live out the goodness that was created in us with our new birth. When I say that, I say more than I understand, and yet the Scriptures make it inescapable. So we can say that in our inner man we *are* good. Our flesh, however, has no good thing in it (see Rom. 7:18). Therefore we must struggle to manifest in our lifestyle the new work that has been done in our spirits, and that includes emulating God by doing good.

The apostle Paul wrote that "glory and honor and peace [go] to every man who does good, to the Jew first and also to the Greek" (Rom. 2:10). In 12:9 he went on to say, "Let love be without hypocrisy. Abhor what is evil; cling to what is good."

In our *relationships* with others we are to do good, and in our *labors* we are to do good. Those are the two areas in which God did good. We try to do things that have desirable properties and are gratifying, enjoyable, beneficial, and morally upright.

The Bible is filled, explicitly and implicitly, with specifics on how we are to do good. Some of the explicit things the Bible tells us about doing good are:

1. We are to do good when we can (see Prov. 3:27).

2. We are not to show partiality in our decision making (see Prov. 24:23).

3. We are to help establish justice in our sphere of impact (see Amos 5:15).

4. We are to love our enemies and pray for them (see Luke 6:27–28).

5. We are to abound in deeds of kindness and charity (see Acts 9:36).

6. We are never to pay back evil for evil to anyone, but overcome evil with good (see Rom. 12:17–19, 21).

7. We are to do good to our neighbor (see Rom. 15:2–3).

8. We are to minister our spiritual gifts for others (see 1 Pet. 4:10).

9. We are to do good to all men, but especially our fellow Christians (see Gal. 6:10).

10. We are to obey authorities over us (see Titus 3:1).

11. We are to prompt and help each other to love and good deeds (see Heb. 10:23–24).

There are many other passages that teach *implicitly* that we should do good:

1. We are to love God with all our heart and soul and mind, and our neighbor as ourselves (see Matt. 22:37–40).

2. We are to do unto others as we would have others do unto us (see Matt. 7:12).

3. We are to take care of our families, both their material and immaterial needs (see 1 Tim. 5:8).

4. We are to share the gospel with others (see Isa. 52:7).

5. We are to give money to finance the ministry (see 2 Cor. 9:7).

6. We are to work at our vocations in a way that pleases Christ (see Col. 3:23).

206 30 Days to Understanding What Christians Believe

7. We are to help those in distress, assuming we have the ability to meet their needs (see Luke 10:30–37).

Of course, we could go on and on because the whole Bible addresses the good we should or could do for others. These lists, however, are representative of the types of things we might consider when pondering the responsibility of doing good. These are only a fraction of the passages that teach the responsibility of doing good. They are a reflection of the character of God. All of life rests on the willingness of people to do good to others. Christians ought to lead the way in this.

> Q. What good are we to do?
> A. We are to _____ the character of Jesus
> in all we do.

3. What are the consequences of doing good?
Both temporal blessings and eternal *rewards*.

CENTRAL PASSAGE: For we shall all stand before the judgment seat of God. For it is written, "As I live, says the LORD, every knee shall bow to Me, / And every tongue shall give praise to God." So then each one of us shall give account of himself to God. (Romans 14:10–12)

The Bible teaches us that, in terms of earning our way into a relationship with God, all our righteousness is as filthy rags (see Isa. 64:6). There are no good works we can do to earn favor with God; however, God still wants us to do good. Hebrews 11:6 tells us, "without faith it is impossible to please God." The apostle John tells us that the first good thing anyone can do to please God is to believe in Jesus and accept Him as one's personal Savior. In the sixth chapter of his Gospel, John records the words of Jesus as He talked with a group of people who had followed Him to the opposite side of the Sea of Galilee after He had fed the five thousand. Jesus said to them,

> "Truly, truly, I say to you, you seek Me, not because you saw signs, but because you ate of the loaves, and were filled. Do not work for the food which perishes, but for the food which endures to eternal life, which the Son of Man shall give to you, for on Him the Father, even God, has set His seal." They said therefore to Him, "What shall we do, that we may work

the works of God?" Jesus answered and said to them, "This is the work of God, that you believe in Him whom He has sent." (John 6:26–29)

This is consistent with the observation someone made that the reason it is impossible to please God without faith is that faith is the only thing we can do and still not do anything. The first work we must do (and the only work we can do to begin to please God) is to believe in Jesus and commit our lives to Him. After that, as we have already seen, God wants us to live a life of good works. Those good works, however, are not done to earn our way into God's favor. Rather, they are done as an expression of gratitude and thanks for what God did for us when we believed in Jesus.

That means the person who never receives Jesus as his personal savior may experience the cause-and-effect rewards of a good life while he lives on earth, but he receives no eternal rewards. He receives only condemnation for having rejected Jesus, for without faith it is impossible to please God. The Christian, however, receives not only God's temporal blessings for doing good in this life, but also an eternal reward from God for his or her good works.

We read in 2 Corinthians 5:9–10, "We have as our ambition, whether at home or absent, to be pleasing to Him. For we must all appear before the judgment seat of Christ, that each one may be recompensed for his deeds in the body, according to what he has done, whether good or bad." The judgment seat, in Greek, is called the *bema;* it is the place where the judges sat during Olympic games. It was from that seat that the winners of the competitions received their rewards.

The apostle Paul mentions this again in Romans 14:10–12:

> But you, why do you judge your brother? Or you again, why do you regard your brother with contempt? For we shall all stand before the judgment seat of God. For it is written, "As I live, says the LORD, every knee shall bow to Me, / And every tongue shall give praise to God." So then each one of us shall give account of himself to God.

This idea is amplified in 1 Corinthians 3:10–15:

> According to the grace of God which was given to me, as a wise master builder I laid a foundation, and another is

building upon it. But let each man be careful how he builds upon it. For no man can lay a foundation other than the one which is laid, which is Jesus Christ. Now if any man builds upon the foundation with gold, silver, precious stones, wood, hay, straw, each man's work will become evident; for the day will show it, because it is to be revealed with fire; and the fire itself will test the quality of each man's work. If any man's work which he has built upon it remains, he shall receive a reward. If any man's work is burned up, he shall suffer loss; but he himself shall be saved, yet so as through fire.

We see from this that, at the judgment seat of Christ, there is no danger of losing one's salvation. If someone has failed to do good works he loses his reward, but he is still saved. In addition, if he has done a good work he will be rewarded for it.

What are the consequences of our doing good? Both temporal blessing and eternal reward.

Q. What are the consequences of doing good?
A. Both temporal blessings and eternal _____.

4. What are the consequences of not doing good?

A more difficult life on earth and eternal *separation* from God.

CENTRAL PASSAGE: This is the work of God, that you believe in Him whom [God] has sent. (John 6:29)

As we said in the previous section, the first "good" thing we are to do is to believe in Jesus. When the apostles asked, "'What shall we do, that we may work the works of God?' Jesus answered and said to them, 'This is the work of God, that you believe in Him whom He has sent'" (John 6:28–29). If we do not do the good thing of believing in Jesus, then the wrath of God abides on us (see Eph. 2:3).

Of course, if we do other good things in this life, we reap the benefits of that; life simply goes better for the person who lives a good life. That is not to say that life goes better for all people who do good than for all people who do not do good. But however anyone's life is going to go, given his life circumstances, it will go better if he is a good person and does good things.

But all that ceases when we die. At that moment, if we have not believed in Christ as our personal Savior, we fall under the eternal condemnation of God (John 3:17–18). When it comes to pleasing God before we are Christians, all our righteous deeds are as filthy rags (see Isa. 64:6). How good we are during our life has nothing whatsoever to do with whether we go to heaven when we die. It all depends on whether we have believed in Jesus, repenting of our sins and giving our life to Him.

When someone dies without having received Jesus, he or she eventually stands before God at what is called the great white throne of judgment:

> And I saw a great white throne and Him who sat upon it, from whose presence earth and heaven fled away, and no place was found for them. And I saw the dead, the great and the small, standing before the throne, and books were opened; and another book was opened, which is the book of life; and the dead were judged from the things which were written in the books, according to their deeds. And the sea gave up the dead which were in it, and death and Hades gave up the dead which were in them; and they were judged, every one of them according to their deeds. And death and Hades were thrown into the lake of fire. This is the second death, the lake of fire. And if anyone's name was not found written in the book of life, he was thrown into the lake of fire. (Rev. 20:11–14)

A person's name is written in the book of life when he receives Jesus as his personal Savior and Lord (see Philippians 4:3), and those who are not found in the book of life at the time of judgment are judged according to their works. They will have rejected the first great work, believing in Jesus, and will be condemned as a result. But within the ranks of those who are condemned, apparently, there are degrees of judgment (see Matt. 10:25) since judgment is based on deeds (see 2 Cor. 5:10). A good man, in the terms of the world, who lived a life of good deeds would experience less severe judgment than the man whose life was given over to evil deeds. But all who do not do the good work of believing in Jesus will not only miss the rewards at the judgment seat of Christ, they also will reap condemnation at the great white throne of judgment.

Q. What are the consequences of not doing
good?
A. A more difficult life on earth and eternal
_____ from God.

Conclusion

To do good is one of the most powerful things in the world.
When one's character is known by doing good, that person becomes a highly esteemed and even powerful person. We all admire
people who do good. We think of Abraham Lincoln, Helen Keller,
Mother Teresa . . . We think of people in our own lives who
are obscure but good: a neighbor, a grandmother, a co-worker.
When we see goodness, it touches us deeply. Why, then, do we
not make a greater attempt to be the kind of people who are
known for doing good?

Perhaps because doing good is unselfish and we are too
insecure to spend time, energy, and resources doing good for
others when we feel we need to spend those things on ourselves.

The challenge of the Scripture and of Christ is that each
of us become committed, not to getting ahead in the world or
to getting comfortable in the world, but to doing good. The irony
is that doing good is the surest way to get ahead or even to get
comfortable in our hearts. Yet we resist it. Don't! Take up the
challenge. Determine to become a person who is known for doing
good to others.

Review

CENTRAL PASSAGE: For we are His workmanship, created in Christ Jesus
for good works, which God prepared beforehand, that we should walk
in them. (Ephesians 2:10)

1. Q. Where does goodness come from?
   A. It is a reflection of the *character* of God.

2. Q. What good are we to do?
   A. We are to *reflect* the character of Jesus in all we do.

3. Q. What are the consequences of doing good?
   A. Both temporal blessings and eternal *rewards*.
4. Q. What are the consequences of not doing good?
   A. A more difficult life on earth and eternal *separation* from God.

Self-Test

1. Q. Where does goodness come from?
   A. It is a reflection of the _____ of God.

2. Q. What good are we to do?
   A. We are to _____ the character of Jesus in all we do.

3. Q. What are the consequences of doing good?
   A. Both temporal blessings and eternal _____.

4. Q. What are the consequences of not doing good?
   A. A more difficult life on earth and eternal _____ from God.

TEN KEY WORDS OF BIBLE DOCTRINE

TWENTY-ONE

FAITH

Faith is the art of holding on to things
your reason has once accepted, in spite
of your changing moods.

C. S. Lewis

DEFINITION OF FAITH: Believing what God has said and acting accordingly.

CENTRAL PASSAGE: And without faith it is impossible to please Him, for he who comes to God must believe that He is, and that He is a rewarder of those who seek Him. (Hebrews 11:6)

The three great theological virtues are faith, hope, and love. These words appear together throughout the Epistles (see Col. 1:4–5, 1 Thess. 1:3, and 1 Pet. 1:3–8), and they reach their pinnacle in 1 Corinthians 13:13: "But now abide faith, hope, love, these three; but the greatest of these is love." It is impossible to look at the key words of Bible doctrine without looking at these three great theological virtues.

Faith is a difficult term to define because it is used in different ways in the Bible. The dictionary definition of faith is, "reliance or trust in a person or thing" (*Oxford American Dictionary*), and that is a good beginning. Hebrews 11:1 defines faith as "the assurance of things hoped for, the conviction of things not seen." The writers of the New Testament used the words *pistis*, which is translated "faith," and *pisteuo*, which is translated "believe."

One thing we know is that, when referring to the primary understanding of faith in the biblical sense, it does not refer merely to intellectual acceptance of something being true. That is, to believe that Jesus lived is not the same thing as having faith in Him. The apostle James wrote, "You believe that God is one. You do well; the demons also believe, and shudder" (James 2:19). So merely believing something to be true, intellectually accepting something as true, is not the same as exercising biblical faith. You exercise biblical faith when, after accepting something intellectually as true, you then act accordingly. You commit yourself to the truth.

An often-told story describes a man who stretched a steel cable over the river at Niagara Falls and walked across the cable and back. Then he took a wheelbarrow and wheeled the wheelbarrow across the river and back. Then he asked how many people believed he could wheel the wheelbarrow across and back with a person sitting in it. All hands went up. But when he asked for a volunteer to sit in the wheelbarrow, no hands went up. They all intellectually assented to the possibility, but none believed deeply enough to act on his belief.

A similar point is made in John 2:23–25: "Now when He was in Jerusalem at the Passover, during the feast, many believed in His name, beholding His signs which He was doing. But Jesus, on His part, was not entrusting Himself to them, for He knew all men." The word *entrusting* is the same as the word *believing*. So from this use of the word we understand that the biblical concept of faith, or believing, includes the idea that we must make a commitment to the thing we believe. We must act on the implications of the thing we say we believe.

I cannot remember a time when I did not believe in the existence of God and Jesus as His Son. Even as a young child I accepted the existence of them both and believed everything about them that needed to be believed. But no one ever told me that I needed, then, to commit my life to them. I did not become a Christian until I was nineteen and in college. It was then that someone made it clear to me how I was to respond to what I believed. I made a commitment of my life to God and His Son, Jesus, and became a Christian. My faith became more than just an intellectual recognition; it became an acceptance and commitment.

So that is faith when it comes to God and Jesus. We must believe *in* them, not just believe that they exist. That is why the Bible says "without faith, it is impossible to please Him" (Heb. 11:6).

But faith goes beyond just believing in God and Jesus. It extends to having faith in what They say. To have faith in what They say means that we (1) Obey it as a command, (2) Rest in it as a promise, and (3) Accept it as a truth and act accordingly.

For example, we may believe that Jesus commanded, "Go into all the world and preach the gospel" (Mark 16:15), and we may accept that as a good thing. But we have not exercised faith until we have actually gone. If we believe that God has a right to command us ("Do you not know that your body is a temple of the Holy Spirit who is in you, whom you have from God, and that you are not your own? For you have been bought with a price: therefore, glorify God in your body" 1 Cor. 6:19–20) but do not do what He has commanded, then we are not entrusting ourselves to Him. We are not committing ourselves to Him unless we obey Him.

In another example, when Jesus gives us a promise, we are not exercising faith unless we rest in that promise. In Matthew 6:25–34, Jesus exhorts us not to worry about tomorrow, what we will eat or wear. God knows our needs and will supply them: "seek first His kingdom and His righteousness; and all these things shall be added to you. Therefore do not be anxious for tomorrow; for tomorrow will care for itself. Each day has enough trouble of its own" (Matt. 6:33–34). If we rest in that promise and don't worry, we are exercising faith. If we don't rest in that promise and if we worry about tomorrow, we are not exercising faith.

This is, of course, easier said than done, and I would not want to imply to anyone that because I say this, I also do it unfailingly. Living by faith is something that must be learned, and just about the time we think we have learned it God teaches us about faith on a deeper level. Then we realize that our previous understanding was shallow and now we have to learn faith on another whole level. There is no end to it.

When it comes to this kind of obedience, we are often like the fellow who fell over a cliff and caught hold of a small branch to keep from plummeting to his death below. He knew he couldn't hang on for long, so he cried, "Help, help! Is anybody up there?"

A great, deep voice said, "Yes, I am here."

"Who is that?" the man asked.

"The Lord," came the reply.

The man cried, "Lord, help me!"

The Lord said, "Certainly. Do you trust me?"

"Of course. I trust you completely," he pleaded.

The Lord said, "Good. Let go of the branch."

"What!?" the man cried.

"Let go of the branch," the voice reiterated.

There was a long pause. Then the man said, "Is anybody else up there?"

When it comes to total obedience to the Lord, most of us want to know if anyone else is up there. But nobody else is. Total obedience to the Lord is the shortest route between us and the life we long for, but only if we trust God completely and we are willing to obey Him completely.

In summary, biblical faith means it is not enough to intellectually accept that something is true. We must commit ourselves to that truth . . . we must live out the implications of the truth. If we don't we are not exercising biblical faith.

Faith extends most obviously to three things: First, accepting who God and Jesus are and entrusting yourself to Them, accepting Their right to rule over your life. Second, believing the commands and instructions in the Scripture and obeying them. Third, believing the promises in the Bible and resting in them.

Another important thing to recognize about faith is that it is a gift of God. Ephesians 2:8–9 says, "For by grace you have been saved through faith; and that not of yourselves, it is the gift of God; not as a result of works, that no one should boast." We see, then, that even the ability to exercise faith is a gift of God. Also, in Galatians 5:22–23, where Paul lists the fruit of the Spirit, he includes *faithfulness*. So whether it is coming to God for salvation or living a life of faith before Him, faith is a gift of God.

From Philippians 2:12–13 we learn that God gives us an initial capacity for faith, and then we are responsible to act on it: "So then, my beloved, just as you have always obeyed, not as in my presence only, but now much more in my absence, work out your salvation with fear and trembling; for it is God who is at work in you, both to will and to work for His good pleasure." When we do act on it, He increases our capacity. He increases, we act; He increases, we act. In this way, we continuously grow in faith. Even though it is a gift of God we must appropriate His gift, and when we do, He gives us more.

I read a wonderful illustration of how faith grows and is strengthened in this way. Many years ago it was decided to put a suspension bridge across a wide gorge. The trick was how to get started. First the bridge builders shot an arrow from one side to the other; the arrow carried a tiny thread across the gulf. Then they tied a piece of twine to the thread and pulled it back across. To the twine on the other side they tied a small rope, pulling that back across. Then they added a larger rope and finally the iron chains from which the suspension bridge was to hang. That is how we grow. When we are faithful and obedient in small things, the Lord increases our capacity and greater things follow. It all begins with the prayer of the disciples: "Lord, increase our faith!"

Review

DEFINITION OF FAITH: *Believing* what God has said and *acting* accordingly.

CENTRAL PASSAGE: And without faith it is impossible to please Him, for he who comes to God must believe that He is, and that He is a rewarder of those who seek Him. (*Hebrews* 11:6)

Self-Test

DEFINITION OF FAITH: _____ what God has said and _____ accordingly.

CENTRAL PASSAGE: And without faith it is impossible to please Him, for he who comes to God must believe that He is, and that He is a rewarder of those who seek Him. (_____ 11:6)

TWENTY-TWO

HOPE

> When you say a situation is hopeless you are slamming the door in the face of God.
>
> Charles L. Allen

DEFINITION OF HOPE: The confident expectation that God will see us through our trials on earth to our home in heaven, and that in the end all will be well.

CENTRAL PASSAGE: May the God of hope fill you with all joy and peace in believing, that you may abound in hope by the power of the Holy Spirit. (Romans 15:13)

Hope is to life as gasoline is to a car. Hope fuels life. Without hope, you cannot go on. Hope is the second of the three great theological virtues, along with faith and love. Just as it is with faith and love, we cannot live without hope.

In his book *Man's Search for Meaning* Victor Frankl argued that the "loss of hope and courage can have a deadly effect on man." As a result of his experiences in a Nazi concentration camp, Frankl contended that when a man no longer possesses a motive for living, no future to look toward, "he curls up in a corner and dies." He wrote, "Any attempt to restore a man's inner strength in camp had first to succeed in showing him some future goal" (*Illustrations for Biblical Preaching,* p. 194).

Hope is a "future" word. Faith, in some limited sense, is a "past" word because it means we believe something that is already true. Hope is a future word in that we look forward to something that is not true yet but we believe will be true in the future. The stronger your hope is in the promises of the Bible, the more peace your life will have. The weaker your hope is in promises of the Bible, the less peace you will have. If you have weak hope you may be plagued with doubt and uncertainty and the anger, fear, or depression that goes along with them. If you have great hope you will be soothed with peace.

Of course, we all vacillate. Few of us have unfailing hope in the promises of the Bible. But that is the goal toward which we can pray and labor. And that is the state in which we will have the greatest peace.

There are at least three areas in which we need hope in this life. First, we need hope that this world makes sense, that there is meaning and purpose behind it. We need hope that God exists and that He is the One who invests creation with meaning and purpose.

From the earlier part of the twentieth century to the present, in academic and scientific circles, the prevailing view of the universe has been that the universe is one gigantic accident. Incredible, to be sure, but an accident. The belief is that there is no God, that there is no absolute truth, and that man is simply the highest being on the scale of evolution. As a result there is no meaning and purpose to life in general, there is no moral standard to which we must all adhere, and there is no heaven and no hell. Therefore we should eat, drink, and be merry, for tomorrow, we die.

The main problem with that view is that while you can eat and drink, it is hard to be merry for long in a life without meaning and purpose.

The apostle Paul wrote, "If we have hoped in Christ in this life only, we are of all men most to be pitied" (1 Cor. 15:19). He also wrote "that which is known about God is evident within [mankind]; for God made it evident to them. For since the creation of the world His invisible attributes, His eternal power and divine nature, have been clearly seen, being understood through what has been made, so that they are without excuse" (Rom. 1:19–20).

If we believe God created the world, and there is greater evidence to suggest that He did than that it was an accident, then suddenly the world takes on meaning and purpose it didn't have before. There is hope that this life has meaning. Therefore there is hope that I have meaning, identity, and worth. With God, there is hope for purpose and personal meaning. Without God, there isn't.

A second area in which we need hope, once we have accepted the first area, is to get through the trials of life. Sometimes life comes in on us like a tidal wave, and we feel hopeless to prevail. It may be confusion and bewilderment over decisions we have to make. It may be intense physical pain. It may be debilitating emotional pain. We may lose a loved one and wonder how we can go on. We may be abandoned by our spouse in divorce. Our children may rebel and reject us. We may have a financial reversal or any other disaster. We in the Western world are largely unable to appreciate the magnitude of the plight of some in the Third World who are trapped in a refugee camp, slowly but surely starving to death while knowing there is enough food somewhere but territorial infighting is keeping the food from getting to them. So they watch their children waste away and look forward only to a slow, painful death.

There is, in the life of some people, unspeakable pain, unimaginable trials. And from time to time, while our trials may not be quite so extreme, they seem extreme to us and overwhelm us. At times like that, we need hope that God will see us through . . . that His grace will be sufficient for all our needs.

To this, the Bible speaks. The apostle Peter wrote, "Therefore, gird your minds for action, keep sober in spirit, fix your hope completely on the grace to be brought to you at the revelation of Jesus Christ" (1 Pet. 1:13). This opens the subject we must grasp if we are to have the grace and strength to cope with life's trials: namely, that this world is not our home. It is a training ground for heaven. As we face the trials of life, we must fix our hope completely, not on anything in this world, but on the next. Peter expanded this idea in 1 Peter 2:11 when he wrote, "Beloved, I urge you as aliens and strangers to abstain from the fleshly lusts which wage war against the soul."

In Hebrews 11:13, we read, "All these [people of great faith] died in faith, without receiving the promises, but having seen them and having welcomed them from a distance, and having confessed that they were strangers and exiles on the earth." We are aliens in this world. We are strangers. If we are to be able to face the present trials of this world we must fix our hope on Jesus. If we fix our hope on this world we are certain to be deeply disappointed. We cannot control the people or our possessions and circumstances sufficiently to fix our hopes on this world; life will overwhelm us.

In his book *Rediscovering Holiness,* James Packer wrote, concerning mediocrity in pursuit of holiness, "I suspect it springs from the folly of not viewing this life as preparation for heaven." We are visitors to this planet. We were meant to dwell with God, but mankind fell. God is in the process of redeeming and reclaiming all who will turn to Him. When we do our task is to prepare for heaven and to share the good news of Christ with others to encourage as many as we can to make the journey with us. We are to manifest the character and proclaim the name of Christ, and we are to use our time on earth to prepare ourselves to meet Him. Anything else is a misplacement of our hope and a misuse of our time. The apostle John said, "everyone who has this hope fixed on Him purifies himself, just as He is pure" (1 John 3:3).

When we turn to Christ in hope for the trials of this life, we are blessed with a strength, a stability, that cannot be known or gained any other way. Hebrews 6:19 says, "This hope we have as an anchor of the soul."

A third area in which we need hope is for life after death. We want to know that when the great conveyer belt of life drops us off at the end we will land someplace safe. Dying is the ultimate experience of being out of control. We want some assurance that since we cannot control events after our death, perhaps someone else can. Hope for life after death is the third great area of hope provided by Christ.

The apostle Paul wrote, "if we have hoped in Christ in this life only, we are of all men most to be pitied" (1 Cor. 15:19). It is hope for life after death, for reward of good deeds, for continued relationship with God and loved ones who are also Christians . . . For all these we have great hope. Paul wrote in Romans 15:4, "For whatever was written in earlier times was written for our instruction, that through perseverance and the encouragement of the Scriptures, we might have hope." And great hope, indeed, we take from the Scriptures. The apostle Peter wrote:

> Blessed be the God and Father of our Lord Jesus Christ, who according to His great mercy has caused us to be born again to a living hope through the resurrection of Jesus Christ from the dead, to obtain an inheritance which is imperishable and undefiled and will not fade away, reserved in heaven for you, who are protected by the power of God through faith for a salvation ready to be revealed in the last time. (1 Pet. 1:3–5)

Based on that hope, Peter encourages us to "hang in there":

> In this [hope] you greatly rejoice, even though now for a little while, if necessary, you have been distressed by various trials, that the proof of your faith, being more precious than gold which is perishable, even though tested by fire, may be found to result in praise and glory and honor at the revelation of Jesus Christ; and though you have not seen Him, you love Him, and though you do not see Him now, but believe in Him, you greatly rejoice with joy inexpressible and full of glory, obtaining as the outcome of your faith the salvation of your souls. (1 Pet. 1:6–9)

Paul also wrote in Romans 8:24–25, "For in hope we have been saved, but hope that is seen is not hope; for why does one also hope for what he sees? But if we hope for what we do not see, with perseverance we wait eagerly for it."

Some years ago a hydroelectric dam was to be built across a valley in New England. The people in a small town in the valley were to be relocated because the town would be submerged when the dam was finished. During the time between the decision to build the dam and its completion, the buildings in the town, which previously had been kept up nicely, fell into disrepair. Instead of being a pretty little town, it became an eyesore.

Why did this happen? The answer is simple. As one resident said, "Where there is no faith in the future, there is no work in the present" (*Illustrations for Biblical Preaching,* p. 194).

Hope is necessary for life; hope fuels life. If you run out of hope, you run out of the ability to keep going in life. The

Scriptures give us hope in three areas: First, hope that this universe is not a great accident, that there is intelligence, purpose, and meaning behind it. Second, that God's grace will be sufficient to get us through the trials of life. Third, that everything will be all right when we die. What hope! What an anchor to hold on to in the storms of life!

Review

DEFINITION OF HOPE: The confident *expectation* that God will see us through our trials on earth to our home in heaven and that in the end all will be well.

CENTRAL PASSAGE:: May the God of hope fill you with all joy and peace in believing, that you may abound in hope by the power of the Holy Spirit. (*Romans* 15:13)

Self-Test

DEFINITION OF HOPE: The confident _____ that God will see us through our trials on earth to our home in heaven and that in the end all will be well.

CENTRAL PASSAGE: May the God of hope fill you with all joy and peace in believing, that you may abound in hope by the power of the Holy Spirit. (_____ 15:13)

TWENTY-THREE

LOVE

Love seeketh not itself to please,
Nor for itself hath any care;
But for another gives its ease
And builds a heaven in hell's despair.

William Blake

DEFINITION OF LOVE: The exercise of my will toward the benefit of another.

CENTRAL PASSAGE: "You shall love the LORD your GOD with all your heart, and with all your soul, and with all your mind." This is the great and foremost commandment. The second is like it, "You shall love your neighbor as yourself." (Matthew 22:37–40)

When we look at love, the third great theological virtue after faith and hope, we must consider two aspects of it. The first is loving God, and the second is loving others. It is important to separate these two aspects because loving God is different than loving others. Our love for God is a response of gratitude for what He has done for us ("We love, because He first loved us," 1 John 4:19). Our love for others is modeled after God's love for us ("The one who loves God should love his brother also," 1 John 4:21).

When we look at the task of loving God, we see that it is in gratitude for what He has done for us, but it also has the central characteristic of obedience. Biblical love for God is not a matter of great emotions sweeping the soul. Though there is nothing wrong with this emotion, one cannot directly control his emotions; therefore, if emotions were involved we could not always control whether or not we love God. God commands us to love

226

Him, and the only thing that can be commanded is the will. Emotions cannot be commanded, but the will can. Jesus said, in John 15:10, "'If you keep My commandments, you will abide in My love; just as I have kept My Father's commandments, and abide in His love.'" The apostle John wrote, "For this is the love of God, that we keep His commandments" (1 John 5:3). That is what it means to love God: to keep His commandments. If we keep God's commandments, we love Him regardless of whether great emotions sweep over our soul. And if we have great emotions sweeping our soul but do not keep His commandments, we are not loving Him.

Yet when it comes to loving our neighbor, it does not mean keeping all *their* commandments. There may be some instances in which that is what it means, but that is surely a minority of the cases.

One time Jesus was asked what needed to be done to inherit eternal life. Jesus answered, "'What is written in the Law?' The man answered, 'You shall love the LORD your GOD with all your heart, and with all your soul, and with all your strength, and with all your mind; and your neighbor as yourself.' Jesus said, 'You have answered correctly; do this, and you will live.'"

But wishing to justify himself, the man who asked the original question said, "And who is my neighbor?" Jesus responded by giving him the example of the Good Samaritan: A Jew was traveling along a deserted part of a road and was mugged. A priest and a Levite passed by but did not help the injured man who had been robbed and left to die. Then a Samaritan came along and helped the man. Of course, Samaritans and Jews did not get along (see Luke 10:25–35).

"Which of these three do you think proved to be a neighbor to the man who fell into the robbers' hands?" Jesus asked. The man said, "The one who showed mercy toward him." Then Jesus told him, "Go and do the same" (see Luke 10:36–37).

This was Jesus' answer to what it means to love others. He said also, "Greater love has no one than this, that one lay down his life for his friends" (John 15:13). Yet not everyone is our friend, and rarely is this kind of love called for. Perhaps more applicable to everyday life is the apostle Paul's description of love in 1 Cor. 13:4–8a:

Love is patient, love is kind, and is not jealous; love does not brag and is not arrogant, does not act unbecomingly; it does not seek its own, is not provoked, does not take into account a wrong suffered, does not rejoice in unrighteousness, but rejoices with the truth; bears all things, believes all things, hopes all things, endures all things. Love never fails.

That is our measure of love when it comes to relating to others.

A more succinct statement was given by Jesus when He said, "Do to others as you would have them do to you" (Luke 6:31 NIV). This is surely one of the most powerful statements ever uttered by the human tongue. If only this one principle were observed most of the horrors of humanity would cease. That is what it means to love.

Said another way, "Love does no wrong to a neighbor; love therefore is the fulfillment of the law" (Rom. 13:10).

James Packer, in his book *Concise Theology*, wrote:

New Testament Christianity is essentially a response to the revelation of the Creator as a God of love. God is a tripersonal Being who shows ungodly humans that the Father has given the Son, the Son has given his life, and the Father and Son together now give the Spirit to save sinners from unimaginable misery and lead them into unimaginable glory. Believing in and being overwhelmed by this amazing reality of divine love generates and sustains the love to God and neighbor that Christ's two great commandments require. (p. 181)

Conclusion

There are heroic examples of love, and there are simple examples of love. Both stem from the same character of the heart. Life does not always give someone an opportunity to love heroically, but when we love consistently in little things, it adds up to heroism.

In a non-war incident many years ago, the North Korean government illegally confiscated the U.S.S. *Pueblo* and held it for some time. Tensions in the world increased dramatically as negotiations and counter-strategies were undertaken. While the world held its breath acts of heroism were going on. The eighty-two surviving crew members were thrown into brutal captivity. In one particular instance, thirteen of the men were required to sit in a rigid manner around a table for hours. Finally the door was violently flung open and a North Korean guard brutally beat the man in the first chair with the butt of his rifle. The next day, as each man sat at his assigned place, the door was thrown open again and the man in the first chair was brutally beaten. On the third day it happened again to the same man. Knowing the man could not survive, another young sailor took his place. When the door was flung open the guard automatically beat the new victim senseless. For weeks, a new man stepped forward each day to sit in that horrible chair, knowing full well what would happen. At last the guards gave up in exasperation. They were unable to beat that kind of sacrificial love *(Illustrations for Biblical Preaching)*.

That was an example of heroic love. Here is an example of simple love: A young woman walked into a fabric shop, went to the counter, and asked the owner for some noisy, rustling, white material. The owner found two such bolts of fabric but was rather puzzled at the young lady's motives. Why would anyone want several yards of noisy material? Finally his curiosity got the better of him and he asked the young lady why she particularly wanted noisy cloth.

She answered: "You see, I am making a wedding gown, and my fiancé is blind. When I walk down the aisle, I want him to know when I've arrived at the altar so he won't be embarrassed."

Such acts of simple love, when consistently combined with other acts of simple love, become heroic. Whether God calls on us for heroic love or simple love, His love "has been poured out within our hearts through the Holy Spirit" (Rom. 5:5), so that we can love as He asks us to, whether it is loving Him or others.

Review

DEFINITION OF LOVE: The exercise of my *will* toward the benefit of another.

CENTRAL PASSAGE: "You shall love the LORD your GOD with all your heart, and with all your soul, and with all your mind." This is the great and foremost commandment. The second is like it, "You shall love your neighbor as yourself." *(Matthew* 22:37–40)

Self-Test

DEFINITION OF LOVE: The exercise of my _____ toward the benefit of another.

CENTRAL PASSAGE: "You shall love the LORD your GOD with all your heart, and with all your soul, and with all your mind." This is the great and foremost commandment. The second is like it, "You shall love your neighbor as yourself." (_____ 22:37–40)

TWENTY-FOUR

GRACE

The doctrines of grace humble a man without degrading him and exalt a man without inflating him.

Charles Hodge

DEFINITION OF GRACE:: The unmerited favor of God, which He extends to mankind.

CENTRAL PASSAGE: For by grace you have been saved through faith; and that not of yourselves, it is the gift of God. (Ephesians 2:8–9)

Grace is not used in the Bible as a technical term; that is, it does not mean exactly the same thing each time it is used. It is a flexible, accommodating little word that must be understood in light of its context. It is a little like our English word *trunk*, which can mean the rear compartment of a car, the nose of an elephant, a large suitcase, or even, in its plural form, swimming wear! We can easily tell by its context what *trunk* means. The same is true with *grace*.

However, in our context, grace does have three primary usages, and we will look at each one of them then make some summary comments.

1. Grace means "a blessing."

Grace can mean a greeting or a parting. We see this frequently in Scripture, especially in the Epistles:

> Paul . . . to all who are beloved of God in Rome, called
> as saints: Grace to you and peace from God our Father and
> the Lord Jesus Christ. (Rom. 1:1, 7)

> Grace to you and peace from God our Father and the Lord
> Jesus Christ. (1 Cor. 1:3)

In 1 Corinthians 1:3, we see *grace* being used in a greeting.
At the end of 1 Corinthians, we see it being used as a parting:
"The grace of the Lord Jesus be with you" (1 Cor. 16:23).

In 2 Corinthians 13:14, we see perhaps the most well known
parting in the New Testament: "The grace of the Lord Jesus
Christ, and the love of God, and the fellowship of the Holy Spirit,
be with you all."

This, then, describes the first use of the word *grace* as a greeting, a parting, or a general statement of goodwill toward another
person.

2. Grace means "unmerited favor."

This is perhaps the best-known use of the word *grace*. The
Scriptures make it clear that man was in a hopeless condition: lost,
without God. But God, because of His love for mankind, did not
leave man in his hopeless condition; He reached out to man with
favor, even though man had not earned that favor and was unable
to do anything to deserve it.

Perhaps the central passage of Scripture that uses this meaning of grace is at the beginning of this chapter: "For by grace
you have been saved through faith; and that not of yourselves,
it is the gift of God" (Eph. 2:8–9).

This is not, however, the only important verse or passage
that champions this theme. Paul brings the understanding of this
dimension of grace to its greatest heights in Romans 5:15–21:

> For if by the transgression of the one [Adam] many died,
> much more did the grace of God and the gift by the grace of
> the one Man, Jesus Christ, abound to the many. And the gift
> is not like that which came through the one who sinned; for
> on the one hand the judgment arose from one transgression
> resulting in condemnation, but on the other hand the free
> gift arose from many transgressions resulting in justification

[being declared righteous]. For if by the transgression of the one [Adam], death reigned through the one, much more those who receive the abundance of grace and of the gift of righteousness will reign in life through the One, Jesus Christ. So then as through one transgression there resulted condemnation to all men, even so through one act of righteousness there resulted justification of life to all men. For as through the one man's [Adam's] disobedience the many were made sinners, even so through the obedience of the One the many will be made righteous. And the Law came in that the transgression might increase; but where sin increased, grace abounded all the more, that, as sin reigned in death, even so grace might reign through righteousness to eternal life through Jesus Christ our Lord.

In this passage, the theme of grace as "unmerited favor" ascends to its lofty heights and reveals to us the heart of God. He was not willing to leave us in our hopeless condition; He loved us too much for that (John 3:16). So even though we had no claim to His goodwill because of anything we had done or because of any inherent merit within ourselves, God brought His grace, His favor, to us.

The theme is reiterated in other important passages. For example:

If it [salvation] is by grace, it is no longer on the basis of works, otherwise grace is no longer grace. (Rom. 11:6)

He predestined us to adoption as sons through Jesus Christ to Himself, according to the kind intention of His will, to the praise of the glory of His grace, which He freely bestowed on us in the Beloved. (Eph. 1:5–6)

3. Grace is "God's divine enablement."

At times, God empowers us to do things that are His will, and this is sometimes referred to as His grace. For example, in 2 Corinthians 12, Paul wrote of a time when he was given a vision of heaven. Then God gave Paul a "thorn in the flesh" (v. 7) to keep Paul from exalting himself. Paul asked the Lord three times to remove the thorn, but finally, the Lord's answer came back: "And He has said to me, 'My grace is sufficient for you, for power is perfected in weakness'" (v. 9). God promised to give Paul the ability to endure the thorn in the flesh, and that ability was described as grace.

We see other passages using grace in the same way.

> And since we have gifts that differ according to the grace given to us, let each exercise them accordingly. (Rom. 12:6)

> According to the grace of God which was given to me, as a wise master builder I laid a foundation, and another is building upon it. (1 Cor. 3:10)

> But by the grace of God I am what I am, and His grace toward me did not prove vain; but I labored even more than all of them, yet not I, but the grace of God with me. (1 Cor. 15:10)

> Let us therefore draw near with confidence to the throne of grace, that we may receive mercy and may find grace to help in time of need. (Heb. 4:16)

We see, then, that *grace* is also used in the sense of "divine enablement."

Conclusion

C. S. Lewis once wrote of his own experience and perception of grace.

> I never had the experience of looking for God. It was the other way round. He was the hunter (or so it seemed to me) and I was the deer. He stalked me like a redskin, took unerring aim, and fired. And I am very thankful that this is how the first (conscious) meeting occurred. It forearms one against subsequent fears that the whole thing was only wish fulfillment. Something one didn't wish for can hardly be that. (C. S. Lewis, *Christian Reflections*, Harcourt Brace, 1956, p. 169)

Review

DEFINITION OF GRACE: The *unmerited* favor of God, which He extends to mankind.

CENTRAL PASSAGE: For by grace you have been saved through faith; and that not of yourselves, it is the gift of God. (*Ephesians* 2:8–9)

Self-Test

DEFINITION OF GRACE: The _____ favor of God, which He extends to mankind.

CENTRAL PASSAGE: For by grace you have been saved through faith; and that not of yourselves, it is the gift of God. (_____ 2:8–9)

TWENTY-FIVE

ATONEMENT

I must die or get somebody to die for me. If the Bible doesn't teach that, it doesn't teach anything. And that is where the atonement of Jesus Christ comes in.

D. L. Moody

DEFINITION OF ATONEMENT: Making up for a deficiency and thereby restoring a broken relationship.

CENTRAL PASSAGE: Therefore, He [Jesus] had to be made like His brethren [us] in all things, that He might become a merciful and faithful high priest in things pertaining to God, to make propitiation [atonement] for the sins of the people. (Hebrews 2:17)

Sin requires the death of the one who sinned. If that is not understood, then the necessity of Christ's death will never be understood. The peril we are in until we receive Christ will never be understood, either, and we will never have sufficient gratitude to God for our salvation. We must understand the link between sin, death, and atonement.

All of us have sinned (see Rom. 3:23). But, as we discussed in chapter 7, we are not sinners because we sin; we sin because we are sinners. We were born sinners, and not one of us is able to live without sinning. David wrote: "Behold, I was brought forth in iniquity, / And in sin my mother conceived me" (Ps. 51:5). This does not mean that David's mother sinned and David was the result of that sin. Rather it means that from the moment of conception, we are all contaminated with sin. It is not that we are incapable of doing good. It is that we are incapable of not doing bad.

Each of us has sinned, so each of us must die because sin requires the death of the one who sins. Romans 6:23 says, "For the wages of sin is death." This death includes eternal separation from God. God is holy and hates sin (see Jer. 44:4 and Hab. 1:13). It is His nature to punish it (see Ps. 5:4–6 and Rom. 1:18, 2:5–9). Therefore, when we sin, we will be punished for the sin unless there is some way this linkage can be broken.

Since each of us has sinned, and since each one who sins must be eternally separated from God, it seems like a hopeless condition. That is why the apostle Paul wrote: "remember that you were at that time [before you received Christ] separate from Christ, excluded from the commonwealth of Israel, and strangers to the covenants of promise, *having no hope* and without God in the world" (Eph. 2:12, italics mine).

Paul also wrote of this condition in the first part of Ephesians 2:

> And you were dead in your trespasses and sins, in which you formerly walked according to the course of this world, according to the prince of the power of the air, of the spirit that is now working in the sons of disobedience. Among them we too all formerly lived in the lusts of our flesh, indulging the desires of the flesh and of the mind, and were by nature children of wrath, even as the rest. (Eph. 2:1–3)

This is the hopeless condition we are in because we all sin, and the wages of sin is eternal separation from God. But listen to this! The next verse in Ephesians 2 begins with two of the most wonderful words in the Bible: "But God"!

> But God, being rich in mercy, because of His great love with which He loved us, even when we were dead in our transgressions, made us alive together with Christ (by grace you have been saved), and raised us up with Him, and seated us with Him in the heavenly places, in Christ Jesus, in order that in the ages to come He might show the surpassing riches of His grace in kindness toward us in Christ Jesus. (Eph. 2:4–7)

What a marvelous passage! This is the light at the end of the tunnel, and it is not a freight train—it is salvation: forgiveness of sin, a lifting of the penalty. But how did it happen? How could it happen? It happened because of atonement.

Jesus did not sin. Therefore He did not deserve to die. But He came to earth and died anyway. Because He did not deserve to die, God was willing for Jesus' death to count for ours. If we would, by faith, believe in and receive Jesus as our Savior, God would allow His death to count for ours and give us His life. In this way we could escape the penalty for sin.

All of this was pictured in the Old Testament, and when we understand that Old Testament picture it helps us to better understand the New Testament reality. In the Old Testament, a series of animal sacrifices were required of the Israelites so their sins could be forgiven. The death of the animal was required by God because He wanted to "picture" the fact that sin required death. When an Israelite sinned, he would take an animal to the priest and lay his hands on the head of the animal. "And he shall lay his hand on the head of the burnt offering, that it may be accepted for him to make atonement on his behalf" (Lev. 1:4). When the sacrifice was performed properly, sins were forgiven. "The priest shall make atonement on his behalf for his sin which he has committed, and it shall be forgiven him" (Lev. 5:10).

The point is that by laying his hands on the head of the animal, the Israelite was symbolically transferring his sins to the animal. Then the animal was killed. This pictured for the Israelite that the animal was enduring the death that should have been incurred by the Israelite, except for the grace of God.

However, the Bible makes it clear that the sacrificial system was a temporary system. The sins could not be ultimately taken away until a perfect sacrifice could be made. The sins were actually left unpunished, God staying His hand of execution because of the faith of those who believed in Him. Romans 3:25 states: "In the forbearance of God He passed over the sins previously committed." That perfect sacrifice was Jesus, the Lamb of God (John 1:29). The death of Jesus took away, once and for all, the sins of those who believed in God.

That is why Hebrews 10:1, 4 says, "For the Law [the sacrificial system] since it has only a shadow of the good things to come and not the very form of things, can never by the same sacrifices year by year, which they offer continually, make perfect those who draw near. . . . For it is impossible for the blood of bulls and goats to take away sins." But Jesus came and offered Himself, once and for all.

> By this [His crucifixion] will we have been sanctified through the offering of the body of Jesus Christ once for all. And every priest [in the Old Testament system] stands daily ministering and offering time after time the same sacrifices, which can never take away sins; but He, having offered one sacrifice for sins for all time, sat down at the right hand of God. (vv. 10–12)

This "sitting down" indicates that His task is complete; He has provided final atonement. All our sins were placed on Christ, and He died with our sins on His shoulders. The apostle Paul wrote, in Colossians 2:13–14:

> And when you were dead in your transgressions and the uncircumcision of your flesh, He made you alive together with Him, having forgiven us all our transgressions, having canceled out the certificate of debt consisting of decrees against us and which was hostile to us; and He has taken it out of the way, having nailed it to the cross.

Conclusion

There is a little chorus which says something like, "He paid a debt He did not owe, I owed a debt I could not pay." It summarizes quite simply the link between sin, death, and atonement: all sin, so all die. Jesus, however, died in our place. He provided atonement for our sins. That is, He made up our deficiency, which we would be unable to make up ourselves. Jesus was both God and man, and because He was both, His death was sufficient for our atonement. If He were not man, he could not have died. If He were not God, it would not have mattered, because His death would not have been sufficient to cover our sin. He died in our place and provided atonement for our sin.

Review

DEFINITION OF ATONEMENT: Making up for a *deficiency* and thereby restoring a broken relationship.

CENTRAL PASSAGE: Therefore, He [Jesus] had to be made like His brethren [us] in all things, that He might become a merciful and faithful high priest in things pertaining to God, to make propitiation [atonement] for the sins of the people. (*Hebrews* 2:17)

Self-Test

DEFINITION OF ATONEMENT: Making up for a _____ and thereby restoring a broken relationship.

CENTRAL PASSAGE: Therefore, He [Jesus] had to be made like His brethren [us] in all things, that He might become a merciful and faithful high priest in things pertaining to God, to make propitiation [atonement] for the sins of the people. (_____ 2:17)

TWENTY-SIX

REDEMPTION

O Love divine, what hast Thou done!
The Incarnate God hath died for me!
The Father's co-eternal Son
Bore all my sins upon the tree!
The Son of God for me that died;
My Lord, my love, is crucified.

Charles Wesley

DEFINITION OF REDEMPTION: To pay the purchase price.

CENTRAL PASSAGE:: In Him we have redemption through His blood, the forgiveness of our trespasses, according to the riches of His grace. (Ephesians 1:7)

The late Donald Gray Barnhouse, former pastor of the venerable Tenth Presbyterian Church in Philadelphia, used to tell a story that pictured redemption. The story went something like this: A young boy was given a toy sailboat for his birthday and treasured it greatly. One day he was sailing it in a pond in one of the city parks when a strong rainstorm came up. The high wind swept the sailboat to the other side of the pond, and the hard rain caused the overflow over the little dam to be high enough that the boat went over it and was swept into the city's water-drainage system. The young boy was heartbroken, but there was nothing he could do. The boat was lost.

Some time later, he was walking down the street past a toy store and looked in the window to see his very own sailboat. He rushed in and told the proprietor that that was his sailboat. "See," he said, "it even has my initials carved into the hull. "I'm sorry, lad," the proprietor said, "someone brought that boat in here the other day and sold it to me. The boat is now mine. It could be a pure coincidence that the initials on the boat are the same as yours. You can have the boat, but you'll have to pay me what I paid for it."

Well, the young boy did not have the purchase price, so he went home even more dejected than before. The boat was his, but he couldn't possess it. It was not fair.

That evening when his father returned home from work, the young boy told him the story. The next day, the father went down to the toy store and bought back the boat which, in fact, belonged to his son. He redeemed the boat. He rescued the boat. He saved and delivered the boat and returned it to its rightful place. "That," says Barnhouse, "is redemption."

Redemption has several dictionary meanings coming from different Greek words that are all translated as "grace." First, it can mean "to purchase from the marketplace." This would be the same word you would use if you were to buy a potato from the local market. The word is *agorazo*, which comes from the word for marketplace. It is used in Revelation 5:9, "Worthy art Thou to take the book, and to break its seals; for Thou wast slain, and didst purchase for God with Thy blood men from every tribe and tongue and people and nation." In relation to our salvation, it means simply to pay the price our sin demanded.

The second word is the same word, *agorazo*, with the prefix *ex* added to it. *Ex* means "out of." So *exagorazo* means, not only to pay the purchase price, but also "to take out of the marketplace." In relation to our salvation, it means that, not only did Christ pay the price for our sin, but He also removed us from the "marketplace" of sin. "Christ redeemed [*exagorazo*] us from the curse of the Law, having become a curse for us" (Gal. 3:13).

The third word is an entirely different word, *lutrao*, which means "to pay a ransom," so that the "held one" can be freed.

> And if you address as Father the One who impartially judges according to each man's work, conduct yourselves in fear during the time of your stay upon earth; knowing that you were not redeemed [lutrao] with perishable things like silver or gold from your futile way of life inherited from your forefathers, but with precious blood, as of a lamb unblemished and spotless, the blood of Christ. (1 Pet. 1:17–19)

When we take all three of these words together to form a composite picture of redemption, we see that with Christ's death on the cross, believers in Him have been (1) Purchased, (2) Removed from the marketplace of sin, and (3) Set free to live a new life.

As the word is used in differing contexts in the Bible it takes on subtle variations in meaning. It can mean "to buy something back," as described in Leviticus 25:25: "If a fellow countryman of yours becomes so poor he has to sell part of his property, then his nearest kinsman is to come and buy back what his relative has sold."

In the Psalms, David tended to use the word in the sense of "to save or deliver": "Redeem Israel, O God, / Out of all his troubles" (Ps. 25:22) and, "But as for me, I shall walk in my integrity; / Redeem me, and be gracious to me" (Ps. 26:11).

In the New Testament, the word sometimes has the sense of rescue, or deliverance:

> But when the fulness of time came, God sent forth His Son, born of a woman, born under the Law, in order that He might redeem those who were under the Law, that we might receive the adoption as sons. (Gal. 4:4–5)

> [Jesus] gave Himself for us, that He might redeem us from every lawless deed and purify for Himself a people for His own possession, zealous for good deeds. (Titus 2:14)

But in each case, whether the word has the connotation of save, or deliver, or rescue, it is done by paying the purchase price for something. That price was, of course, the death of Jesus, substituted for our own through the exercise of our faith in Him.

No one on earth could pay the price for another person because the one who would volunteer to do so would, himself, deserve to die. A loving husband or father might want to die to pay the price for a wife or child. But since the husband or father would himself deserve to die because of his own sin, his death could not be substituted for another's. In Psalm 49:7 we read, "No man can by any means redeem his brother, / Or give to God a ransom for him."

The only one who could pay the price for another's death is someone who did not deserve to die. The only person who ever lived who fit that description is Jesus. Because He was a perfect man, He could die in the place of another. Because He was God, His death had infinite measure . . . that is, it could count for countless others. His death can be a substitute for as many as believe in Him and receive Him as their personal Savior. Jesus can redeem all who will come to Him.

Conclusion

The story is told of an orphaned boy who was living with his grandmother when their house caught fire. The grandmother, trying to get upstairs to rescue the boy, died in the flames. The boy's cries for help were finally answered by a man who climbed an iron drainpipe and came down with the boy hanging tightly to his neck.

Several weeks later, a public hearing was held to determine who would receive custody of the child. A farmer, a teacher, and the town's wealthiest citizen all gave the reasons they felt they should be chosen to give the boy a home. As they talked, the boy's eyes remained focused on the floor.

Then a stranger walked to the front and slowly took his hands from his pockets, revealing the scars on them. As the crowd gasped, the boy cried out in recognition. This was the man who had saved his life and whose hands had been burned when he climbed the hot pipe. With a leap the boy threw his arms around the man's neck and held on for dear life. The other men silently walked away, leaving the boy and his rescuer alone. Those marred hands had settled the issue.

Review

DEFINITION OF REDEMPTION: To pay the purchase *price.*

CENTRAL PASSAGE:: In Him we have redemption through His blood, the forgiveness of our trespasses, according to the riches of His grace. (*Ephesians* 1:7)

Self-Test

DEFINITION OF REDEMPTION: To pay the purchase _____.

CENTRAL PASSAGE:: In Him we have redemption through His blood, the forgiveness of our trespasses, according to the riches of His grace. (_____ 1:7)

TWENTY-SEVEN

REGENERATION

I was twenty years old before I ever heard a sermon on regeneration. I was always told to be good, but you might as well tell a midget to be a giant as to tell him to be good without telling him how.

D. L. Moody

DEFINITION OF REGENERATION: Being spiritually reborn in holiness and righteousness.

CENTRAL PASSAGE: He saved us, not on the basis of deeds which we have done in righteousness, but according to His mercy, by the washing of regeneration and renewing by the Holy Spirit. (Titus 3:5)

When people discuss what it means to be a Christian the discussion often ranges from what one believes to how good one must be in his or her lifestyle. One thing is certain: A Christian is someone to whom something very specific has happened. Before this thing happens to him he is *not* a Christian, and after this thing has happened to him he *is* a Christian. This "thing" is that he is regenerated. Jesus described it as being born again. We listen in on His discussion with Nicodemus in the third chapter of the Gospel of John. Nicodemus was a member of the elite religious ruling party, and he came to Jesus by night to talk with Him. In the course of the conversation, Jesus told Nicodemus that he must be born again. Nicodemus's next question was rhetorical. He said, "Why, how can a man be born again? He cannot enter into his mother's womb a second time and be born, can he?" Jesus answered him with a rebuke. He said, "Are you a teacher of Israel, and you don't know the answer to that? We are all born once physically, and that makes us a member of this earthly kingdom. But My kingdom is spiritual, and to be a member of My spiritual kingdom, you must be born again *spiritually.*"

Now, of course, all of that is a paraphrase of John 3 combined with commentary, but it is the gist of the conversation. A spiritual rebirth is necessary to become a Christian. Before you have that spiritual rebirth, you are not a Christian. After you have that spiritual rebirth, you are. That is regeneration. Our dead spirits are regenerated. Paul wrote in Ephesians 2:1, "And you were dead in your trespasses and sins." In what way were we dead? Physically? Obviously not. Dead people don't read letters from other people. Paul meant they were spiritually dead.

He went on in verses 4 and 5 to say, "But God, being rich in mercy, because of His great love with which He loved us, even when we were dead in our transgressions, made us alive together with Christ." That is what it means to be born again. It means to be made alive spiritually.

After that spiritual rebirth, we are changed from life to death (Eph. 2:5), we are transferred from the kingdom of darkness to the kingdom of light (Col. 1:13), we are given eternal life in exchange for eternal death (Eph. 2:1–10), and we are given bondage to righteousness in exchange for bondage to unrighteousness (Romans 6). That is what happens when we are regenerated.

It comes as a surprise for many people to learn that how good you are as a human being (in comparison, of course, to other human beings) has nothing whatsoever to do with whether you go to heaven. Even the best person is not good enough; we simply cannot get there by being good. No, when it comes to going to heaven, the issue isn't "goodness." The issue is "perfection." And since no one is perfect, no one can get to heaven based on his or her own merit. No matter how many good works you pile on top of your first sin, they don't take away your first sin. That is why you must be born again to get to heaven. The old self must die, and a new self must be born again.

To illustrate this principle, imagine you are a manufacturer of glass windows for airplanes. The government comes to you with a contract to make the windows in the space shuttle. The demands on the glass for the space shuttle are much greater than they are for an airplane. Much greater stress is placed on windows for the space shuttle than on airplane windows. You go over your manufacturing capabilities and decide you can do it, but the window must be perfect. Any imperfection automatically disqualifies it.

Let us imagine that you make the first window, and it is not perfect. It has one small blemish in the upper right-hand corner. You tell the government inspector that the window is 99.9 percent perfect. It only has one small flaw, so small no one would even notice it. You announce with great pride that the rest of the glass is perfect, and you also make the point that the flaw occurred early on in the manufacturing process. Since that time, no other flaws occurred. From the remainder of the manufacturing process, to transportation, to installation, the window had no more flaws. It was installed in the shuttle with no other incidents.

Despite all that the government inspector would, of course, disqualify the window. After the first flaw nothing else matters. The first flaw disqualifies it, because the issue isn't whether the window is good. The issue is whether the window is perfect. The fact that the imperfection occurred early on is also irrelevant, as are the facts that the flaw is small and the installation process went without a hitch. Only one thing is relevant: The window is not perfect. It wouldn't matter if it had one crack or a hundred, the window cannot be uncracked. The only solution is a new window. A perfect window.

The same is true with us and sin. We are born with sin. We sin because we are sinners. Some of us sin a little, and some of us sin a lot, but we all sin. So the only thing that can be done is to get a new window . . . that is, for our old self to die (which it did in Christ, see Romans 6) and to be born again to newness of life in holiness and righteousness, in the very likeness of God, which it is (see Eph. 4:24).

That is regeneration. That is what it is, and that is the necessity for it. Before a person is regenerated, he or she is not a Christian. After a person is regenerated, he or she is a Christian.

Conclusion

One man has written:

We may sweep the world clean of militarism, we may scrub the world white of autocracy, we may carpet it with democracy and drape it with the flag of republicanism. We may hang on the walls the thrilling pictures of freedom: here, the signing of America's Independence; there, the thrilling portrait of Joan of Arc; yonder, the Magna Carta; and on this side the inspiring picture of Garibaldi. We may spend energy and effort to make the world a paradise itself where the lion of capitalism can lie down with the proletarian lamb. But if we turn into that splendid room mankind with the same old heart, deceitful and desperately wicked, we may expect to clean house again not many days hence. What we need is a peace conference with the Prince of Peace. (Arthur Brisbane, cited in *Illustrations for Biblical Preaching*, p. 300)

The world is as it is because men are not regenerated. While it is true that society does have a corrupting influence on people, those people first created the society. We will never change the world until we change men's hearts, and the only way to do that is through regeneration by the Holy Spirit.

Review

DEFINITION OF REGENERATION: Being spiritually *reborn* in holiness and righteousness.

CENTRAL PASSAGE: He saved us, not on the basis of deeds which we have done in righteousness, but according to His mercy, by the washing of regeneration and renewing by the Holy Spirit. (*Titus* 3:5)

Self-Test

DEFINITION OF REGENERATION: Being spiritually _____ in holiness and righteousness.

CENTRAL PASSAGE: He saved us, not on the basis of deeds which we have done in righteousness, but according to His mercy, by the washing of regeneration and renewing by the Holy Spirit. (_____ 3:5)

TWENTY-EIGHT

JUSTIFICATION

Though the mills of God grind slowly,
Yet, they grind exceeding small;
Though with patience He stands waiting,
With exactness grinds He all.

Henry Wadsworth Longfellow

DEFINITION OF JUSTIFICATION: Being declared righteous by God.

CENTRAL PASSAGE: Therefore, having been justified by faith, we have peace with God through our Lord Jesus Christ. (Romans 5:1)

The Evangelical Dictionary of Theology defines *justification* as "to pronounce, accept, and treat as [righteous], and not . . . liable, and, on the other hand, entitled to all the privileges due to those who have kept the laws." It declares a "verdict of acquittal, and so excluding all possibility of condemnation. Justification thus settles the legal status of the person justified." It makes a person, as has been commonly said, "just as if I'd never sinned."

Being declared righteous by God seems initially to be an impossibility to any thinking Christian. How can someone who sins be declared righteous? It is an apparent contradiction that stymies logical thought—until a deep look is given at some key passages of Scripture.

The issue of justification has divided Christians for centuries. It was the central dividing issue between Catholics and Protestants during the Reformation, and it even divides people today. The trouble often surrounds the issue of sin and whether or how much a Christian can sin and still maintain his or her salvation. The flip side of that is, of course, the issue of how

249

righteous persons can sin. Does God look the other way when we sin? Does He pretend he doesn't see? Does He not "sweat the small stuff"? Doesn't He care about white lies and blind spots? How can God declare us righteous if we sin?

In addressing this conundrum, we must first begin by establishing the fact that God does, indeed, declare us to be righteous. Our central passage states it in no uncertain terms: "Having been justified by faith, we have peace with God through our Lord Jesus Christ." How are we justified? Paul stated it earlier in Romans 4:2–3: "For if Abraham was justified by works, he has something to boast about; but not before God. For what does the Scripture say? 'And Abraham believed God, and it was reckoned to him as righteousness.'"

This passage tell us that justification brings about righteousness. We are justified, and all God's children have always been justified by faith.

James Packer, in his book *Concise Theology*, states it concisely:

> God's justifying judgment seems strange, for pronouncing sinners righteous may appear to be precisely the unjust action on the judge's part that God's own law forbade (Deut. 25:1, Prov. 17:15). Yet it is in fact a just judgment, for its basis is the righteousness of Jesus Christ who as "the last Adam" (1 Cor. 15:45), our representative head acting on our behalf, obeyed the law that bound us and endured the retribution for lawlessness that was our due and so (to use a medieval technical term) "merited" our justification. So we are justified justly, on the basis of justice done (Rom. 3:25–26) and Christ's righteousness reckoned to our account (Rom. 5:18–19).

It is as the songwriter wrote:

> No merit of my own His anger to suppress.
> My only hope is found in Jesus' righteousness.

When we believe in Jesus and receive Him personally as our Savior, our sins are forgiven, we are born again, and Jesus' righteousness becomes ours. This is very difficult to explain, and when we attempt it we get all tangled up with the chapter on regeneration. But we will try.

When we are born again, it is our spirit that is reborn. Our body is not reborn, as Nicodemus correctly observed in John 3. Our reborn spirit is born in the likeness of God, created in righteousness and holiness of the truth (Eph. 4:24). Paul called this the "inner man" in Romans 7, and refused to attribute any sin to it (Rom. 7:20). This inner man, this reborn spirit, is righteous. It is the flesh that sins (again, Romans 7). Paul stated that we eagerly await our complete adoption as sons, namely the redemption of our bodies (Rom. 8:23). So our redemption has two stages. The first stage is when our spirit is redeemed and born again. This spirit is holy and righteous. Our body isn't redeemed, and it is not holy and righteous. Therefore, in a way that exceeds our wisdom or understanding of Scripture, a civil war wages within a person between his "inner man" (Rom. 7:22) and the flesh.

So when the Bible says we are declared righteous, it does so on two grounds. First it is on the grounds, as Packer said, that Jesus is our head. He has already lived perfectly accordingly to the Law so that He did not deserve to die. Then He died in such a way that God was willing to allow His death to count for ours if we would but believe in Him and follow Him in faith. Then everything that will happen at the final judgment (forgiveness of our sin and confirmation in total righteousness) is brought forward, in the mind of God, to the moment of our salvation.

But the second grounds on which God declares us to be righteous is that He is looking at our spirit when He declares us righteous; He is not looking at our body, our flesh. Our spirit is righteous, just as righteous as if we had never sinned. One day, when God completes our redemption by giving us new bodies untouched by sin, our redemption will be complete.

So we see that God does not slyly look the other way when we sin. He recognizes that the sin is in our flesh, our unredeemed body, not in our spirit. Not one more thing has to happen to the spirit before we go straight to heaven, except to receive a sinless body.

What happens when we are justified? Well, as we have already seen, we have peace with God (see Rom. 5:1). We are saved from God's wrath through Christ (see Rom. 5:9). We are glorified (see Rom. 8:30). We become heirs, having the hope of eternal life (see Titus 3:7).

Nothing we can do will make us righteous before God. As Paul wrote in Galatians 2:16, "A man is not justified by the works of the Law but through faith in Christ." In Titus 3:5–7, we read:

> He saved us, not on the basis of deeds which we have done in righteousness, but according to His mercy, by the washing of regeneration and renewing by the Holy Spirit, whom He poured out upon us richly through Jesus Christ our Savior, that being justified by His grace we might be made heirs according to the hope of eternal life.

We are justified by faith, that is, declared righteous, because we *are* righteous in Christ.

Conclusion

Merlin Carothers, author of the book *Prison to Praise,* had firsthand experience of what it is like to be declared righteous. During World War II, he joined the army. Anxious to get into some action and impatient with his slow-moving unit, Carothers went absent without leave but was caught and sentenced to five years in prison. Instead of sending him to prison, though, the judge told him he could serve his term by staying in the army for five years. The judge told him if he left the army before the five years ended, he would have to spend the rest of his sentence in prison. Carothers was released from the army before his five-year term had passed, so he returned to the prosecutor's office to find out where he would be spending the remainder of his sentence. To his surprise and delight, Carothers was told that he had received a pardon from President Truman. The prosecutor explained: "That means your record is completely clear, just as if you had never been involved with the law" (*Illustrations for Biblical Preaching,* p. 207).

Review

DEFINITION OF JUSTIFICATION: Being declared *righteous* by God.

CENTRAL PASSAGE: Therefore, having been justified by faith, we have peace with God through our Lord Jesus Christ. (*Romans* 5:1)

Self-Test

DEFINITION OF JUSTIFICATION: Being declared _____ by God.

CENTRAL PASSAGE: Therefore, having been justified by faith, we have peace with God through our Lord Jesus Christ. (_____ 5:1)

TWENTY-NINE

SANCTIFICATION

In regeneration we pass out of death into life, but in sanctification, we pass out of the self-life into the Christ-life.

A. B. Simpson

DEFINITION OF SANCTIFICATION: The process of spiritual growth toward the character image of Christ.

CENTRAL PASSAGE: This is the will of God, even your sanctification. (1 Thessalonians 4:3 KJV)

Sanctification is the process of spiritual growth toward the character image of Christ. It is the will of God for all His children, as we saw in our central passage.

Regeneration is solely the work of God. We, of course, must believe in Jesus and receive His offer of salvation, but after that the process of regeneration is wholly His (Titus 3:5). In contrast, sanctification requires a mutual interplay between the initiating work of God and the responding work of man (even though man's response, his willingness to respond, and his ability to respond are gifts of the Holy Spirit).

Perhaps the central passage in Scripture that describes this process is Philippians 2:12–13:

> So then, my beloved, just as you have always obeyed, not as in my presence only but now much more in my absence, work out your salvation with fear and trembling; for it is God who is at work in you, both to will and to work for His good pleasure.

We see from this passage that God works in us to will, or to desire, His good pleasure. He also works in us to *work* for His good pleasure. We, however, must respond. We must obey, as Paul said in Philippians 2:12. The Westminster Shorter Catechism defines sanctification as "the work of God's free grace, whereby we are renewed in the whole man after the image of God, and are enabled more and more to die unto sin, and live unto righteousness" (question 35).

Sanctification must be understood in two ways from its use in Scripture. There is *positional sanctification*, which means we are permanently "set apart" for God. That happened when we were born again; it is now complete and needs no further action (Acts 26:18). Then there is *progressive sanctification*, which is the moral and spiritual renewal, growth, and renovation whereby we are changed more and more into the character image of Christ. This is the meaning of sanctification that we are focusing on in this chapter. It is dependent upon our response to the work of the Holy Spirit within us. First Corinthians 6:11 says, "And such [sinners] were some of you; but you were washed, but you were sanctified, but you were justified in the name of the Lord Jesus Christ, and *in the Spirit of our God*" (italics mine).

This thought is continued in 1 Corinthians 6:19–20, where we read, "Or do you not know that your body is a temple of the Holy Spirit who is in you, whom you have from God, and that you are not your own? For you have been bought with a price: therefore, glorify God in your body."

Perhaps the strongest statement is found in 2 Corinthians 3:18: "But we all, with unveiled face beholding as in a mirror the glory of the Lord, are being transformed into the same image from glory to glory, just as from the Lord, the Spirit." So there we have it. The Lord, the Spirit, is at work transforming us into the image of the Lord. That process is sanctification.

As we saw from Philippians 2:12–13, the Lord initiates and we respond, and even when we respond the Spirit must strengthen us. Jesus said, "Apart from Me you can do nothing" (John 15:5).

It is important to emphasize, because of the difficulty of maintaining balance in this area, that sanctification is neither all of God nor all of us. We have the two extremes of "let go and let God" on the one hand, and "do everything yourself" on the other. In reality, sanctification is a process of our interacting with the Lord, in relationship with Him, to achieve a spiritual maturity that transforms us into the character image of Jesus. It is a process in which both God and man must be at work. And this work He promises to do,

> [that]you may walk in a manner worthy of the Lord, to please Him in all respects, bearing fruit in every good work and increasing in the knowledge of God; strengthened with all power, according to His glorious might, for the attaining of all steadfastness and patience. (Col. 1:10–11)

God has committed Himself to the sanctification process, and He calls upon us to do the same (see Rom. 12:1–2 and 2 Tim. 2:15).

The standard to which God calls us in sanctification is His own perfection, His own holiness (of which we will speak more in the next chapter), His own law. We strive to keep His moral law, not in order to gain acceptance with Him, because we gained acceptance with Him in Christ when we received His Son into our lives by faith. But we strive to keep His moral law out of gratitude that He accepted us in spite of our inability to keep His moral law.

All of this is terribly complicated by a civil war that rages within us. The spiritually reborn "inner man" (Rom. 7:22) desires only to do good. But the power of the flesh within us prompts us to do evil (Rom. 7:18–23). This conflict will rage within us until we die and receive the new bodies, untouched by sin, that will complete our redemption (Rom. 8:23). Yet there are ways that we can gain, rather than lose, in the battle:

1. As Jesus said, "Keep watching and praying, that you may not enter into temptation; the spirit is willing but the flesh is weak" (Matt. 26:41).

2. Consciously give yourself over to Christ as a living sacrifice. Paul said, in Romans 12:1–2:

> I urge you therefore, brethren, by the mercies of God, to present your bodies a living and holy sacrifice, acceptable to God, which is your spiritual service of worship. And do not be conformed to this world, but be transformed by

the renewing of your mind, that you may prove what the will of God is, that which is good and acceptable and perfect.

3. Maintain an eternal perspective on this life and live for the next:

> If then you have been raised up with Christ, keep seeking the things above, where Christ is, seated at the right hand of God. Set your mind on the things above, not on the things that are on earth. For you have died and your life is hidden with Christ in God. (Col. 3:1–3)

By cultivating disciplines that strengthen the role of the Spirit and weaken the role of the flesh in your life, you gradually experience the transformation of character that is sanctification.

How long will it take? It always seems to take a little longer than is reasonable. Part of this is explained by the impatience that is normal in this situation, such as the little boy who wants to grow more quickly so he can play basketball or drive the car or sail the boat. Another reason is that one's consciousness of sin will always remain ahead of his or her lifestyle; we can always see farther down the road than we are. The more like Christ we become, the more clearly we can see our weaknesses, our limitations, our sins. In a sense, the more holy we become, the more we realize we are not holy. Keep in mind that the process is not expected to be completed in this life; we will never experience sinless perfection. But we can always be in a state of growing into the character image of Christ.

Conclusion

One of the most difficult areas for some people to bring under the Lordship of Christ is their driving habits. If you are one of those who cannot seem to get control over the habit of speeding, an exercise that might help you is to sing hymns while you are driving. If you are going a certain speed, you might sing a certain hymn reflecting the safety of each speed. For example:

45 miles per hour—"God Will Take Care of You"

55 miles per hour—"Guide Me, O Thou Great Jehovah"

65 miles per hour—"Nearer, My God, To Thee"

75 miles per hour—"Nearer, Still Nearer"

85 miles per hour—"This World Is Not My Home"

95 miles per hour—"Lord, I'm Coming Home"

100 miles per hour—"Precious Memories"

Another sign of the ongoing process of sanctification is the buttons that some Christians wear that bear the letters "PBPGINFWMY." They stand for "Please be patient. God is not finished with me yet." And He isn't. But one day you will be a work of art to His glory.

Review

DEFINITION OF SANCTIFICATION: The process of spiritual growth toward the *character* image of Christ.

CENTRAL PASSAGE: This is the will of God, even your sanctification. (1 *Thessalonians* 4:3 KJV)

Self-Test

DEFINITION OF SANCTIFICATION: The process of spiritual growth toward the _____ image of Christ.

CENTRAL PASSAGE: This is the will of God, even your sanctification. (1 _____ 4:3 KJV)

THIRTY

HOLINESS

How little people know who think that holiness is dull. When one meets the real thing it is irresistible. If even 10 percent of the world's population had it, would not the whole world be converted and happy before the year's end?

C. S. Lewis

DEFINITION OF HOLINESS: Personal purity.

CENTRAL PASSAGE: But like the Holy One who called you, be holy yourselves also in all your behavior; because it is written, "You shall be holy, for I am holy." (1 Peter 1:15–16)

Anyone who gains even a small grasp of the holiness of God and His call on us to be holy will be sobered by it. To grasp that God is holy can be not only sobering but even a frightening thing. To grasp that He calls us to be holy can be the same. His grace assures us that we are His children yet, as C. S. Lewis implied in *The Chronicles of Narnia*, God is not safe. What Lewis meant by that is that His holiness and His desire for us to be holy will often extract from us a price that we, if we *could*, would choose not to pay. We find the price too intimidating. But often in God's severe mercy He does not give us the option of avoiding it. His love for us is that great. Again, as Lewis put it in *The Chronicles of Narnia*, "Aslan [Lewis's animal metaphor for God in the fantasy story] is not a safe lion."

Yet sobered or intimidated though we may be by it, holiness as it relates to us is a primary, perhaps *the* primary, occupation of God. We must understand holiness if we are to understand what God is doing in our lives.

Holiness is

> the word that signifies everything about God that sets him apart from us and makes him an object of awe, adoration, and dread to us. It covers all aspects of his transcendent greatness and moral perfection and thus is an attribute of all his attributes, pointing to the "Godness" of God at every point. Every facet of God's nature and every aspect of his character may properly be spoken of as holy, just because it is. The core of the concept, however, is God's purity, which cannot tolerate any form of sin (see Hab. 1:13) and thus calls sinners to constant self-abasement in his presence (Isa. 6:5). (James Packer, *Concise Theology*, p. 43.)

We must distinguish between imputed holiness and practiced holiness. When we were born again, we were made holy in our spirit (see Eph. 4:24). The great task of the Christian life is to live out in our fallen bodies this righteousness that has already been created in our spirits. Therein lies the internal civil war we have mentioned before. But when God calls us to be holy, He is not calling on us to correct any defect created in our inner man when He caused us to be born again in holiness and righteousness (see Romans 7). Rather, He is calling on us to match our external behavior with the internal righteousness we received in Christ when we received Him as our personal Savior.

When He calls us to be holy, He is calling us to match our behavior with His. This, of course, we cannot do. So how do we respond to His call to be holy as He is holy? Is He calling us to something that is impossible for us? In one sense yes, because we will never reach sinless perfection in this life. But in another sense, His call to us is not out of reach because His grace has made it possible.

In all the Bible, Isaiah 6:1–8 is the central chapter about our holiness as it relates to God's holiness. I will present our study of this passage in four parts so we can gain some understanding of how we are to respond to God's call for holiness.

Part 1, Isaiah 6:1–4:

> In the year of King Uzziah's death, I saw the Lord sitting on a throne, lofty and exalted, with the train of His robe filling the temple. Seraphim stood above Him, each having

six wings; with two he covered his face, and with two he covered his feet, and with two he flew. And one called out to another and said,

> Holy, holy, holy is the LORD of hosts,
> The whole earth is full of His glory.

And the foundations of the threshold trembled at the voice of him who called out, while the temple was filling with smoke.

Part 2, Isaiah 6:5:

> Then I said,
> "Woe is me, for I am ruined!
> Because I am a man of unclean lips,
> And I live among a people of unclean lips;
> For my eyes have seen the King, the LORD of hosts."

Part 3, Isaiah 6:6–7:

> Then one of the seraphim flew to me, with a burning coal in his hand which he had taken from the altar with tongs. And he touched my mouth with it and said, "Behold, this has touched your lips; and your iniquity is taken away, and your sin is forgiven."

Part 4, Isaiah 6:8:

> Then I heard the voice of the Lord, saying, "Whom shall I send, and who will go for Us?" Then I said, "Here am I. Send me!"

These verses tell us something about the holiness of God and how we can respond properly to it. In Part 1, Isaiah saw a vision of the Lord in His holiness. He was in the temple; He was lofty and exalted. Mighty angels attended Him, and smoke filled the temple.

In Part 2, when Isaiah saw God's holiness, he felt a deep sense of his own sin, and he repented deeply. He feared because he knew that being in the presence of God could cost him his life. He acknowledged his sin and the sin of the people among whom he lived.

In Part 3, when Isaiah repented deeply, God forgave deeply, cleansing him with burning fire. It often takes burning fire in our lives to bring us to repentance and to cleanse us of besetting sin or to take us to a new level of spiritual maturity.

In Part 4, when Isaiah had been forgiven because of his repentance, he was usable by the Lord. Two things are worth noting in Part 4. First, when God asked who would go it seemed self-evident to Isaiah that he would go. He did not say, "Well, if you can't find anyone better, I will go." He didn't say, "I can't go. I'm not good enough." He knew he was a sinner, but he knew God had done a significant thing in his life. He had seen the Lord in a new way, and it brought him to a deeper level of repentance than ever before. He understood that this was the way God's demand for holiness was satisfied and that he was usable.

The second thing to observe is that when Isaiah volunteered the Lord did not say, "Who, you?! You've got to be kidding! I don't need a man of unclean lips to serve Me." Rather, He took Isaiah at his word. When Isaiah volunteered the Lord immediately took him up on it and gave him his commission (v. 9).

Practical holiness is rooted in repentance. When we are called to holy living, the fear we may have is that God expects us never to sin again. That places a burden on us that no one can bear. The issue is not that we will never sin again; the issue is that there is an appreciation for holiness and that when sin occurs, repentance follows. There is no other way for a person to live a holy life before the Lord than to be a person of ready repentance. He must sharpen and cultivate his understanding of the holiness of the Lord. As he does, he will gain a clearer sense of his own practical unholiness. This will drive him to deeper and deeper repentance, which will make him more and more usable by the Lord. Following the pattern in Isaiah 6, an appreciation for the holiness of God reveals personal sin. When personal sin is repented, the person is ready for service.

Conclusion

Oswald Chambers once said, "God has one destined end for mankind—holiness! His one aim is the production of saints. God is not an eternal blessing-machine for men. He did not come to save men out of pity. He came to save men because He had created them to be holy" (*Inspiring Quotations,* p. 88). If that is true, then we lean into God's plan, not away from it. We make the fundamental decision that we will accept God's desired destiny for us: to be holy. We say, alarming as it may be for us to hear our own words, "I will be holy." It does not mean we will never sin again. It means we live a life of ready repentance. God can use whoever is ready to repent deeply, be forgiven deeply, and used greatly.

Review

DEFINITION OF HOLINESS: Personal *purity*.

CENTRAL PASSAGE: But like the Holy One who called you, be holy yourselves also in all your behavior; because it is written, "You shall be holy, for I am holy." (*1 Peter* 1:15–16)

Self-Test

DEFINITION OF HOLINESS: Personal _____.

CENTRAL PASSAGE: But like the Holy One who called you, be holy yourselves also in all your behavior; because it is written, "You shall be holy, for I am holy." (_____ 1:15–16)

Congratulations! You have finished a formidable task, and now you have a framework for adding to your knowledge of Bible doctrine. As I said at the beginning, this book is not intended to be the last of your study of the great subjects and words of Scripture, but rather the beginning. May God bless you as you pursue the truth that will set you free!

TEN
GREAT
DOCTRINES
OF
SYSTEMATIC
THEOLOGY
(CHART)

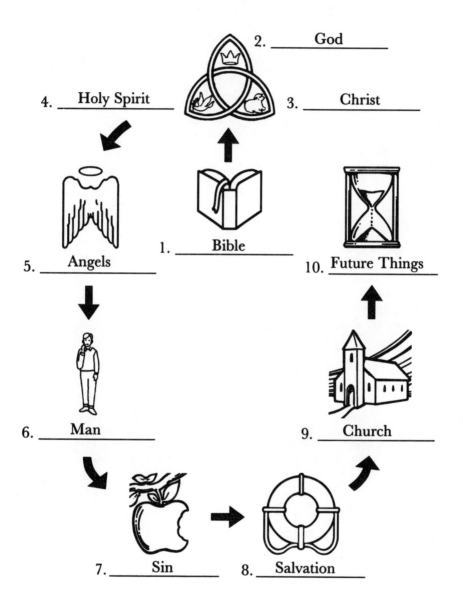

2. _____ God _____

4. _____ Holy Spirit _____

3. _____ Christ _____

1. _____ Bible _____

5. _____ Angels _____

10. _____ Future Things _____

6. _____ Man _____

9. _____ Church _____

7. _____ Sin _____

8. _____ Salvation _____